Rethinking
ASIA

Education and Innovation

Rethinking Asia
Education and Innovation

4th Edition May 2, 2017
Copyright © 2017 by Center for Asia Leadership Initiatives
Printed in Seoul, Korea

A Publication of the Center for Asia Leadership Initiatives
Acumen Publishing
14 Nancy Lane Waltham MA 02452 USA

Center for Asia Leadership Initiatives
Website: www.asialeadership.org
Facebook: www.facebook.com/asiagroup

Asia Leadership Trek
Website: www.asialeadershiptrek.org
Facebook: www.facebook.com/asialeadershiptrek
Twitter & Weibo: @Asia_Trek

Library of Congress Control Number 2017938909
KDP ISBN: 978-1-5212706-9-1
US $13.99

For inquiries on partnership or sponsorship, or purchase of the publication,
please email us at: cali@asialeadership.org

Education and Innovation

*Essays by Harvard University and Tufts Fletcher students
who journeyed through 13 cities in 9 countries in Asia*

RETHINKING

ASIA

1

edited by John Lim & Hungsoo S. Kim
4th Edition

ACUMEN™
PUBLISHING

To all the aspiring leaders of this world

| Table of Contents |

•••

Part 3 • Epilogue

| About the Editors |

•••

Hungsoo S. Kim, a Korean national, is the Co-founder and President of the Center for Asia Leadership Initiatives. Passionate about nurturing and empowering talents in Asia, he has been actively engaging various stakeholders in developing and running over twenty-five programs in more than twenty-two countries in Asia to help emerging leaders explore opportunities to be socially responsible in facing the region's complex challenges. These programs fall under the Center's four main initiatives, namely the Asia Leadership Trek, a public diplomacy arm for scholars at Harvard, Stanford, MIT, and Fletcher; the Asia Leadership Institute, a leadership capacity-building arm; the Acumen Case Center, a research and content development arm; and Acumen Publishing, a publication arm. Hungsoo oversees these initiatives, along with a team of twenty comprising Faculty and Teaching Fellows from Harvard and Stanford University, and administrators at the main office in Boston, U.S., and the Asian regional headquarters in Kuala Lumpur, Malaysia.

As part of his continuous endeavor toward grooming leaders of tomorrow, Hungsoo recently joined the Asia Future Institute, a Seoul-based policy and leadership think tank, as Executive Director to instill in Korean and Northeast Asian talents the drive and passion to create positive social change through effective leadership. He prides himself on accelerating efforts to reach out to all forty-eight countries in Asia by 2022. Hungsoo's areas of research and training, among others, include 'Negotiation and Mediation,' 'Adaptive Leadership,' 'Persuasion and Influence,' and 'Creative Confidence.' To date, some twenty-five thousand burgeoning and established leaders from the government, non-profits, and corporate world in Asia have benefited from these programs.

Prior to establishing the Center, Hungsoo worked for twelve years in varying sectors from strategy consulting and social entrepreneurship to international development, politics, and government. He has also served as a policy aide in the United Nations in New York representing Korea, and as a project analyst at UNESCO in Paris. He currently sits on the board of two non-profit organizations, and has served as a visiting scholar at the Asia Center at Harvard University and at the Kellogg School of Management in Northwestern University. Hungsoo holds a Masters of Public Administration from the Harvard Kennedy School of Government; Masters in International Cooperation from the Graduate School of International Studies, Seoul National University; and completed his undergraduate studies with two majors in U.S. and International Law, and International Politics with a minor in Economics from Handong University.

John Lim is Co-founder and Managing Director of CALI Boston. A former fellow of the Harvard University Asia Center, he has worked in diverse organizations including the Embassy of Canada in Korea, the International Crisis Group, and in different sectors such as English education and social entrepreneurship. His current work engages him in researching and applying various leadership, education, and entrepreneurial models and frameworks within the Asian contexts.

| About the Contributors |

•••

Hungsoo S. Kim is the Co-founder and President of the Center for Asia Leadership Initiatives. Passionate about nurturing and empowering talents in Asia, he has developed and organized over twenty-five programs in more than twenty-two countries in the region to help budding leaders enhance their leadership competencies to navigate challenges in the 21st century. Hungsoo aims to engage with youth in all forty-eight countries in Asia by 2022 and inspire them to enact change in the world.

John Lim is the Co-founder and Managing Director of CALI Boston. He holds a Masters of Arts in Law and Diplomacy from the Fletcher School of Law and Diplomacy and the Graduate School of International Studies, Yonsei University.

Zhoulai Zhu is a graduate of the Harvard Graduate School of Education. Born and educated in China, she has developed an interest in bettering language education in China and has published several articles on English online education in Chinese national academic journals. Before her time at Harvard, she worked in various educational positions, including teaching Mandarin in a British International School, teaching English in a Chinese public school, and working for NGOs in Southeast Asia. Zhoulai currently works as the Director of School Outreach and Partnership at InGenius Prep in Shanghai and New Haven.

Margaret McKenzie is a Master's degree graduate in Law and Diplomacy at the Fletcher School at Tufts University. Her work focused on water, security studies, negotiation, and conflict resolution. She conducted her research in Kuwait as a Boren Fellow in 2015. Prior to her studies at Fletcher, Margaret served as an Information and Communications Officer at USAID in Washington, DC. She has also worked in Amman, Jordan for a youth development NGO. She is originally from Washington, DC. Margaret currently works as the Kuwait Researcher at Natural Resource Governance Institute in New York.

Raymond Ko obtained his Ph.D. in Neuroscience at Harvard University, investigating the neural circuits underlying the execution of motor sequences. He has been a board member of several organizations at Harvard, including the Graduate Business Club and the Hong Kong Society. He grew up in Hong Kong and earned a Bachelor of Science degree at Tsinghua University, Beijing, and he continues to keep an eye on economic development and business opportunities in China. Raymond currently works as the Manager of Strategic Pricing and Marketing at T-Mobile.

Rachel Loh obtained a Master's degree in Public Policy at the Harvard Kennedy School of Government. Possessing a keen interest in public policy, she believes that each sector—government, business, and civil society—should be able to create and capture value by working collaboratively under strong economic policies. Her convictions stem from working in the Singaporean government for nine years, on both the Tourism and the Economic Development Boards. Rachel currently works as the Director of Strategic Planning & Incentive Policy at Singapore Tourism Board.

Karol Mark Yee is a Fulbright Scholar and earned his Masters of Education degree in the International Education Policy Program at the Harvard University Graduate School of Education. Prior to his time at Harvard, he served as Legislative Affairs Officer at the Senate of the Philippines, his native country, under Hon. Edgardo J. Angara, Chair of the Committee on Education. He also worked as teacher, research assistant, and technology integrator at Xavier School, a K-12 school in Greenhills, San Juan, in the Philippines. Today, Mark works as the Program Director of K-12 Transition Program at the Commission on Higher Education of the Office of the President of the Philippines.

Nikki Skovran is a graduate of the Harvard Business School and has had a distinguished career in both the public and the private sector, where she worked for Procter and Gamble as an engineer. While at Harvard, Nikki embarked on an HBS FIELD experience in Johannesburg, South Africa where she was impressed with the entrepreneurial energy; she worked with the Awethu Project, a startup incubator that exchanges business skills training for equity stakes in new ventures. Following graduation at Harvard, she took up a position at Bain and Company in Sydney, Australia. She is originally from Pennsylvania.

Paul Yoo, a Korean-American, studied at the Harvard Graduate School of Education. He has worked for a private educational enterprise, Interpark Paedea, for which he led multiple projects in language research, program development, and program implementation. He has also run an independent education project in the rural province of East China and is now expanding upon that model with an alternative school in South Korea. He aspires to explore and shape the role of higher-education institutes in fostering decision-making skills in students. Paul currently works as the Project Associate at RAND Corporation in Santa Monica, California.

Zach Przystup has a Master's degree from The Fletcher School of Law and Diplomacy at Tufts University, where he studied U.S. Foreign Policy, Pacific Asia, and International Security. Prior to his time at Fletcher, he worked as the U.S. Program Manager at Atlas Corps, where he managed the Atlas Corps Fellowship for thirty-five rising leaders from twenty-three countries. He is from Fairfax, Virginia, and is interested in pursuing a career in government or journalism. He is from Fairfax, Virginia. Today, Zach works as the Associate Director of the Office of Executive Education at the Fletcher School of Law and Diplomacy, Tufts University.

Lars Ragnar Aalerud Hansen is a diplomat with the Norwegian Foreign Service. He spent a year as a Fulbright Scholar at the Fletcher School of Law and Diplomacy at Tufts University, earning a Master's degree in International Relations. Before coming to Fletcher, he completed postings with the Organization for Security and Co-operation in Europe (OSCE) and with the Norwegian Embassies in Moscow, Russia, and Baku, Azerbaijan. He holds a BA in Russian studies from the University of Oslo and completed officer's training at the Norwegian Defense Intelligence and Security School. Lars currently holds a position at the Norwegian Ministry of Foreign Affairs as the Senior Advisor.

| Foreword |

•••

Asia has shown tremendous economic and political growth over the last several decades, which has generated great interest in learning about and truly understanding the many opportunities and challenges in Asia. A number of books have been published that present an analysis of quantitative data on these issues. This is not one of those books. In contrast, this book is unique in that it tries to go behind and beyond these numbers by capturing the immersion of young leaders from around the world on a Trek across several Asian countries to meet with senior political leaders, high-level company managers, and a cross-section of local citizens, as well as to visit historical and cultural venues. The goal of this book is to explore the underlying trends and future directions of these people and their respective countries.

Led by Hungsoo S. Kim, President, and John Lim, Chief Program Director of the Asia Leadership Trek, seventy-six Trekkers embarked on a trip across Asia. The Trekkers both learned from Asian leaders and presented ideas from their perspective. They came from various backgrounds including medicine, academia, government, education, law, international organizations and non-profits. Rather than being tourists, the Trekkers learned to see things from local perspectives, with guidance from country-specific colleagues who joined each leg of the journey. Together, the group met with leaders across Asian countries including Shanghai, Hong Kong, Singapore, Kuala Lumpur, Seoul for four weeks in January and another four weeks in June through Tokyo, Seoul, Beijing Yangon, Bangkok, Jakarta and Bali. These Treks are usually held twice or three times throughout the year; this book compiles experiences across two treks made in 2014. Through a robust framework, ideas were exchanged and best practices were communicated on topics such as entrepreneurship, education and leadership.

This book represents a culmination of a journey - a set of experiences across the Asian continent. The book itself is divided into three parts: History and

Philosophy, New Perspectives and Epilogue. Each chapter is presented from a personal viewpoint of a subgroup of the Trekkers. For the Center for Asia Leadership Initiatives (CALI), which runs the Trek, this is but one of a number of initiatives that bridges East and West, as well as North and South. Following the Trek, fellowships and internships allowed Trekkers to explore specific localities in greater depth for a longer time period. Other CALI activities include the Trilateral Leadership Summit, the Leadership & Innovation Conference and the Redefining Success Conference. The Center also receives support from a number of partners, affiliates and donors such as the Harvard Kennedy School's Ash Center for Democratic Governance and Innovation, and the Harvard University Asia Center.

In summary, what makes this book unique is its novel approach. It brings forth a first-hand look at U.S. and Asia through the lens of the next generation of global leaders. It tells that story of a highly select group of early career leaders from Harvard, MIT and Tufts Fletcher who took a Trek across a number of Asian countries. I hope you can live vicariously through the experiences of these intrepid Trekkers.

Enjoy the journey!

Jay Rosengard, Ph.D.
Adjunct Lecturer in Public Policy
Senior Advisor, Rajawali Foundation Institute for Asia
Ash Center for Democratic Governance and Innovation
Harvard Kennedy School of Government

Part 1

:

History and Philosophy

Chapter 1

Planting the Seed:
How the Asia Leadership Trek Started

Hungsoo S. Kim, Co-Editor
MPA, Harvard Kennedy School of Government

● ● ●

As the early-morning fog rolled off the buildings along the Charles River, I made my daily passage to the Harvard Kennedy School (HKS). I was in a dreamlike state, the kind of feeling you have when your mind and senses are still buzzing from experiencing something significant but you cannot make sense of it yet. I was pondering how I would make use of the eight-day whirlwind trip to Korea I had returned from only days earlier.

This was not an ordinary trip; rather it was an ambitious socio-economic and political tour, in HKS parlance a "trek." Thirty-two HKS graduate students from fourteen different countries participated in this particular "Korea Trek," in March 2012. A longstanding staple of the HKS student experience, the trek is an experiential journey of a country, in which students directly investigate political, economic, industrial, and societal issues through engagement with relevant leaders and organizations. As these treks take place during the school's breaks, they usually last from a week to ten days.

Now, having experienced one of these treks for myself, I analyzed the many facets of what it offered. First, it was a forum that allowed trekkers to connect with influential leaders in a variety of fields, including government, business, and academia. Given the high-ranking positions of many of these leaders, it would not have been possible as an individual traveler to arrange appointments with them. We had meetings with officials from the Blue House (Korea's equivalent to the White House), CEOs of Korea's major corporations, and the heads of think tanks.

Second, the Trek offered not only a top-level view of the country but also a down-to-earth, grassroots perspective of the diverse challenges and opportunities faced by individuals, media organizations, and local communities. We were able to engage with journalists from the *New York Times, Arirang*, and *CNN*, as well as with students and young professionals. After the trip, many Trekkers described how valuable these interactions were in helping them understand the underlying values and mindsets embedded in Korean society.

Third, the participants in the Trek effectively formed a mobile think tank. With thirty-two students from fourteen different countries, all engaged in on-the-ground experiential learning, we were able to capture and test new ideas through the constant exchange of knowledge and insights among the Trekkers themselves.

As valuable as what we learned from each other was the opportunity to interact with the local community. Through a half-day knowledge forum for high school students and a community service program for college student volunteer workers, the Trekkers had the opportunity to give back to Korean society by practicing what they had learned at Harvard through the act of teaching. Individuals in the local community were thus able to take advantage of the knowledge, training, and life lessons of exceptional individuals who were enrolled in the world's most renowned school of public policy.

The programs we held included a panel on leadership; a lecture on economic, political, and social trends in the 21st century; and sessions of career counseling and mentorship. Through these events, the locals we worked with increased their knowledge and received encouragement and inspiration to contribute to their own society. Local students remarked how surprised they were to find that people from Harvard—which many of them viewed as the pinnacle of success—often came from backgrounds different from what they considered "successful." Several of the trekkers, for example, who were exceptional in the areas of finance or medicine, also came from non--profit backgrounds and used their talent in some of the world's most challenging settings. The time spent with the trekkers challenged local participants' assumptions about success and allowed them to gain new perspectives of their future and the larger world.

Thus, as trekkers, we gained a unique and unforgettable learning experience, and at the same time we were able to engage in meaningful public service. The experience was something I did not want to give up. Considering the obvious benefits it had for Harvard students, as well as for the local community in Korea, I began to ask myself how the trek's potential could be expanded and fulfilled.

Southeast Asia Trek: Steps Forward

Only weeks after returning from the Korea Trek, I found an opportunity to advance that vision. After discussions with an old friend, John Lim, who would become my long-time collaborator, I reached out to three HKS students: Alvin Oo from Singapore, Fuadi Pitsuwan from Thailand, and Tram Le from Vietnam, all three of whom joined our team and helped to organize an ambitious, seven-country Southeast Asia Trek for the summer of 2012.

Despite having only two months to plan, we were able to arrange over seventy meetings in seven countries in Southeast Asia: Vietnam, the Philippines, Singapore, Malaysia, Thailand, Myanmar, and Laos. Such a trip was something that had never been done before, an epic socioeconomic smorgasbord that would keep the group of Trekkers away from home for nearly a month. It was the first study trek at HKS to include so many countries and cover such a lengthy period. The group consisted mostly of mid-career students from the Harvard Kennedy School, including an incumbent U.S. state house representative, an attorney, and a management consultant.

Southeast Asia is of growing importance as a region populated by emerging markets that are on the verge of leading global economic growth. Yet all of these markets are susceptible to stagnation, or what is called the "middle-income trap," due to several factors, including weak institutions, corruption, and low educational standards. On the Trek we investigated the way in which Singapore escaped this trap to achieve one of the highest per capita GDPs in the world. Though it is a city state, Singapore and its rise still provided insight when we compared it to Thailand, the Philippines, and Malaysia, countries that have not lived up to their economic potential. Myanmar and Vietnam also offered the Trekkers a look into formerly closed economies whose consumers are now the most optimistic in the region. At the time of our journey, Thailand, Myanmar, and Malaysia were all either undergoing or expected to undergo fundamental shocks to their power structure. As organizers, we wanted the Trekkers to get a sense of what that was like — in other words, to experience democracy in Southeast Asia as it evolved — by listening to the stories of regular people living in the region.

To gain an understanding of the many issues faced by these countries, we arranged meetings with high-profile officials, politicians, and business and non-profit leaders, who provided the Trekkers with nuanced insights into the problems and challenges in their countries. We had the privilege of visiting and engaging in discussions at the Fulbright Economics Teaching Center in Ho Chi Minh, the Asian Development Bank, the Philippine House of Representatives, the Ateneo de Manila School of Government, the Economic Development Board of Singapore, the Lee Kuan Yew School of Public Policy, the Central Bank of Thailand, Air Asia, Siam Cement Group, CIMB Bank, Maybank, and Proton, among others. Aside from meeting the CEOs, academics, and researchers from these organizations, we also met distinguished political leaders like ASEAN (Association of Southeast Asian Nations) Secretary General Surin Pitsuwan, as well as Singapore Deputy Prime Minister Tharman Shanmugaratnam, Malaysia Defense Minister Dr. Ahmad Zahid Hamidi, and Philippine Speaker of the House Feliciano Belmonte.

With about seventy official meetings, two knowledge-sharing events, and extensive historical and cultural sightseeing, the Southeast Asia Trek was an invaluable way for students to learn about a diverse and complex region. To have access to leading political and business figures and engage in learning opportunities in not just one but seven countries is something that under normal circumstances only foreign ministers would be able to experience. It was a once-in-a-lifetime journey for the Trekkers, and the feedback we receive to this day about the trip is filled with such adjectives as "eye-opening," "life-transforming," "rewarding," and "truly amazing."

One of the highlights of the Trek was the series of special programs we hosted for local participants. During our visit to Santa Lucia High School in the Philippines, the local students prepared a program especially for us that featured a creative presentation of their student government as well as a song-and-dance number (and a dance tutorial for a few select Trekkers). In return, we provided a mentoring session, encouraging them to remain committed to their goals and to pursue their dreams.

During this journey, my ideas about the potential of treks as learning experiences began to pick up momentum towards real action. Discussions among the Trekkers ranged from educational methods that equip students with skills for the 21st century, to the lack of courage and adaptability in public leadership, to rising youth unemployment and the need for training and mentorship, to the lack of meaningful and effective engagement in social responsibility initiatives in Asia. The Trek community became fertile ground in which like-minded individuals could offer ideas and test assumptions about their experiences. It became, in effect, an ecosystem in which to plan and carry out our initiatives. John and I agreed to immerse ourselves in a variety of social profit initiatives that would strategically and effectively address issues prevalent in Asia. We concluded that we needed a mechanism to institutionalize our ideas, one that could incorporate the two goals of experiential learning and meaningful public service. Eventually, these discussions acted as the spark that led to a planning initiative and finally to a full-fledged, trek-based program.

Asia Leadership Trek: The Fruits of Our Labor

In the summer of 2013 we began planning another trek to Asia, this time on a much greater scale and with a much more formal structure. Joined by Nur Aziz, a graduate of the Harvard Graduate School of Education, we engaged in many rounds of spirited discussions. Finally we selected our destinations: Shanghai, Hong Kong, Singapore, Kuala Lumpur, and Seoul, in a trip that would cover areas of both Southeast and Northeast Asia.

Over a period of three weeks, in January 2014, the Trekkers would explore these regions through the lenses of public leadership, education, and entrepreneurship. In early discussions, we feared that these three themes might be too disparate. Then, however, we discussed the ideas of a course at HKS called "Policy for Competitiveness," in which the professor argued that education is a key factor in the development of public leadership, which in turn is the biggest factor in fostering strong institutions and a strong talent base. Such institutions drive entrepreneurship, which addresses societal needs and drives growth. Our discussions helped us to see the strong links between the three themes of our program. Under their aegis, our Trekkers would investigate how Asia can better prepare its citizens for the 21st century.

We also decided to include students not only from the Harvard Kennedy School but also from the Harvard Graduate Schools of

Education, Business, and Arts and Sciences, as well as from the MIT Sloan School of Management and the Fletcher School of Law and Diplomacy at Tufts University. We ended up with thirty-four Trekkers from seventeen different countries, who together held a wealth of experience ranging from medicine to law, international development to finance, management consulting to education. Ms. Athena Lam, a program manager at SOW Asia and a social-impact investor who co-organized our forum on leadership and social innovation in Hong Kong, later remarked that one of the draws in working with the Asia Leadership Trek was the interdisciplinary nature of the group. The challenges that societies face today cannot be solved through one lens. New strategies and new ideas are needed from all sectors in order to design innovative and effective solutions for social improvement.

The Asia Leadership Trek program was divided into three-parts: pre-Trek leadership training, the Trek itself, and post-Trek reflection and documentation. Using our two pillars of experiential learning and public service as a foundation, we created a philosophical framework of "mutual sharing." The pre-Trek program addressed our second goal of providing a service opportunity for Trekkers. We organized capacity-building workshops in the areas of leadership, entrepreneurship, and education, which were led by Harvard professors, course assistants, and outside experts. Through attending these workshops and drawing on their coursework and their own areas of expertise, the Trekkers prepared their own workshops, which they would conduct for local communities during the conferences we held during the Trek.

Trekkers were also required to attend community sessions throughout the semester, which helped to form them into one cohesive body in advance of the trip. We used these meetings to work out the logistics of the trip and to prepare for the nearly one hundred meetings, two full-scale conferences (in Malaysia and Korea), and two forums (in Shanghai and Hong Kong) that we held on the Trek.

Pre-Trek

Conference Preparation:	Team-Building:
Workshops	Community Sessions

We also organized smaller country groups and working groups within the Trek. Every Trekker belonged to a country group, in which they helped to plan and organize a particular city's events and talked about issues specific to their assigned country. Every Trekker also belonged to a working group, which helped to organize the diverse activities of the program. The social media team created and shared information on what the Trekkers did to prepare for their journey and what they wanted locals to gain from the Trekkers' visits. The workshop team focused on organizing workshops throughout the semester before the Trek and provided planning and support for the conferences and forums during the Trek. The fundraising team sought sponsors to fund the program. Finally, the book team discussed how the overall experience of the Trek could be creatively chronicled. Each of the members in the book team chose to focus on one or more countries and identified particular issues in that country to explore.

The Purpose of This Book

Since the Southeast Asia Trek, both John and I have regretted losing the chance to document all the stories, lessons, and insights we gained through it. Many times during that Trek, we strongly identified with the sentiments of Mr. Fuadi Pitsuwan, one of the other organizers, who remarked after a meeting with the Deputy Prime Minister of Singapore, "I think I learned more in that one meeting than I did in a whole year of finance class."

These feelings of enlightenment eventually fade when one grasps for memories without the discipline of intentional reflection. The abundance of encounters, one after another, sometimes seemed like an overflowing bucket that we could not control or drink from. Educational theorist John Dewey once said, "We do not learn from experience…we learn from reflecting on experience." How could we capture the lessons and insights of upcoming Asia Leadership Treks, so that they would not spill over and go to waste?

This book is the partial answer to that problem. Along with a fellow Trekker, Lars Hansen, John and I faced the daunting task, after returning from the Trek in late January 2014, of coordinating the writing and publishing of this book within the span of a few months. The authors of each chapter met to discuss and reflect upon the Trek, carving out slices of their experiences and insights from our time in Asia. We did not want the value of our experiences to escape us: by making sense of our crowded memories, we wanted to make the most of our learning. And because academic writing is often inept at conveying emotions and communicating insights, we agreed to write personal essays in a creative, free style, without formal academic rhetoric, in a way that could reflect our own voices.

Although the Trek was a collective experience, the essays in this book do not reflect one perspective regarding Asia. Each of the nine authors comes from a different background and holds a view specific to him or herself. As a result, on certain issues this book offers a wide range of subjective views, some of which directly conflict with each other.

Zhoulai Zhu in her piece, "Shanghai: A City of Two Worlds," offers a measured but optimistic view of China's current status in the political, educational, and business realms. Her foil is Margaret Mc-Kenzie, who is concerned with the long-term costs of development in China and offers a cautionary perspective in "Shanghai: The Price of Development." Raymond Ko, who experienced firsthand China's exam-based education system, discusses the importance of creativity and educational innovation in "Discovering Creativity in Asia." Rachel Loh reflects on the Singapore Miracle — its rapid rise to become one of the wealthiest countries in the world — in "Singapore: A Nation in Transition," examining how the citystate's accomplishments will be tested in the 21st century. Mark Yee, a Filipino, describes the lessons he gained on the Trek and contemplates what they might mean for his home country in "The Questions We Ask: Stories of Efficacy and Resilience." Nikki Skovran, a student at the Harvard Business School, interviewed three entrepreneurs on the Trek and offers an inspiring interpretation of Malaysia's entrepreneurial ecosystem in "Meeting the Heroes in Malaysia." Paul Yoo, a Korean-American, finds a strong connection between the lives of young Koreans and those of young Hong Kongers in "The Desires and Frustrations of Young Asians." Zach Przystup, a student of International Affairs, while discussing his encounters in Shanghai and Seoul in "People-to-People Connections in a Transforming Asia" delves into the deeper meaning of public diplomacy. Lastly, Lars

Hansen, in his chapter, "Asia at the Crossroads: Avoiding Stagnation and Meeting New Challenges," concludes with an overview of each of the cities we visited; he finds that each of the countries is exhausting the potential of the Asian miracle, and speculates on the imminent second remaking of Asia.

The novelist Eudora Welty once wrote, "One place understood helps us understand all places better." Through a profound, analytical exploration of our experiences on the Asia Leadership Trek in January 2014, we seek to bring insight to the varied and complex forces impacting Asia in the 21st century. We hope that through our writing we can provide for you not only a better understanding of different countries and peoples, but also an avenue towards a better understanding of your own setting.

| Chapter 2 |

Mutual Sharing:
The Framework and Philosophy of the Trek

Hungsoo S. Kim and John Lim, Co-Editors

● ● ●

In early December 2013, we looked at our laptop screens with amazement. We had put up only a few online notices for the 2014 summer Trek, and yet within a short period we had received over thirty online applications to add to the nearly forty-three that were still on the waiting list from the winter Trek. With all the preparations still to be done for the winter Trek, which was starting in only a few weeks, we knew there would be even less sleep for us in the next few days. We, along with returning organizer Mr. Fuadi Pitsuwan and new recruit Mr. Andi Sparringa, spent hours poring over these applications, which eventually numbered over one hundred and fifty.

What kind of criteria should one use to determine who stays and who goes? It's often impossible to know who the ideal candidates are, especially when one is deciding between the high-achieving individuals who make up the Harvard, Tufts Fletcher, and MIT Sloan communities. Virtually every candidate we considered was a good candidate, and we thus had to make difficult decisions. We looked for individuals from a variety of backgrounds, who had strong leadership backgrounds and desired to take on leadership roles in the Trek. Secondly, we looked for people who could bring skills and expertise to our workshops and conferences but who were also curious, humble, and eager to learn, particularly about Asian affairs. Finally, we looked for students who were passionate about making a difference in the local communities of Asia. The successful candidates needed to be people who could strongly represent not only the Asia Leadership Trek but their schools, their countries, and themselves.

Why was there such a huge demand for this program? We believe the answer is because we were providing something that the Harvard Kennedy School (HKS) was lacking. Though several of the centers at HKS conduct research on Asia and collaborate with Asian institutions, there was a relative lack of courses solely on Asia. Secondly, though HKS offers a few programs that actively apply skills learned in the classroom to the real world—such as the "HKS Leadership Service Seminar Project," in which students travel to New Orleans, Washington, D.C., or New York City; "Leadership for a Livable City," in which students travel to New York City; "Winter Field Study Course in the Middle East"; and "Community Recovery: Rebuilding Disaster Damaged Communities in Chile"—these experiential programs are few and far in between. More strikingly, all of them in the past have focused on places other than Asia. Thus, for individuals interested in gaining firsthand exposure to Asia and putting into practice in an Asian setting what they've learned in the classroom, there was a huge gap in HKS's offerings.

By developing the Asia Leadership Trek, we were participating in a larger movement in the Harvard community towards more experiential learning. In 2011, the Harvard Business School (HBS) implemented Field Immersion Experiences for Leadership Development (FIELD), a program that "gives students meaningful opportunities to act like leaders, translating their ideas into practice." All first-year students at HBS are now required to travel to an emerging market—often at the far corners of the globe—and work with partner organizations on-site. HBS Dean Nitin Nohria explains some of the obvious benefits of this kind of learning: "We...want to have people make a difference in the world...by giving them this possibility to think about [it] through doing, to have a taste of the difference they can make, even while they're students: they can go to a foreign country and actually do something valuable... They can do something that has the prospect of being real."

How did this philosophy affect us as we developed the Asia Leadership Trek? As mentioned, we first organized a pre-Trek program, which prepared Trekkers with capacity-building programs and included workshops in leadership, entrepreneurship, and education. Among the workshops offered were "Leading Social Change" by HKS Lecturer Jorrit de Jong, "Designing 21st Century Learning Systems" by former Massachusetts Secretary of Education Paul Reville, and "Strategic Impact: Education Entrepreneurship," jointly taught by Harvard Graduate School of Education Professor Monica Higgins and Asian Women's Leadership University President Barbara Hou. Trekkers received advice from these Harvard mentors, who in turn shared their expertise and advised Trekkers on how to adapt and improve the workshops they would be conducting in Asia.

Once on the Trek, acting as a team of teachers and instructional designers, we helped workshop participants in cities all over Asia to apply theoretical frameworks and concepts to their own experience and learning. We thus put into practice what we had learned and studied at our home universities, adapting it to specific audiences in different regions of Asia. We were able to connect with a diverse range of university students and young professionals through instruction, discussion, and inspiration. As Harvard Professor William Kirby said, "the act of teaching in and of itself is an act of practicing what you have learned or studied."

The Trek also allowed us to investigate political, economic, and social issues firsthand, requiring us to experience for ourselves the responsibilities and mindsets of diplomats and journalists in our meetings with political, educational, and entrepreneurial leaders.

Whether it was arranging and conducting meetings with such high-profile leaders such as the President of the Legislative Council of Hong Kong, Parliamentarians in Singapore, opposition-party members in Malaysia, and presidential secretaries in Korea, members of our group acted like the ambassador, the counselor, the first secretary, and the advance coordinating team, all working as one unit. We had to pay close attention to the delicate nature of optics, to seating arrangements, to the suppression of nerves, to the formalities of titles, and to the subtleties of asking questions in a range of sensitive political contexts. The extent of the learning we gained through the process of planning these meeting, as well as the interactions themselves, is incalculable.

At times we also acted as a team of investigative journalists assessing an array of primary data sources one after the other, constantly on the edge of learning. We engaged in dialogues at schools and universities like Fudan High School, the Lee Shau Kee School of Creativity, the School of Science and Technology in Singapore, and the Lee Kuan Yew School of Public Policy, as well as at companies that included the Frog Design Company, Samsung, Hyundai, and Citibank, and at think tanks and consulting firms like the Future-Moves Group, the Asan Institute of Policy Studies, and the North Korea Strategy Group. At all of these places we asked sustained, probing questions on the challenges they faced relating to business and industry, creativity, politics, and public policy. We had to make the most of our limited time with these leaders in order to gain insights about the complex issues affecting their organizations. Afterwards, through discussions in buses and hotel lobbies across Asia, we compared the responses we had received from different countries, different sectors of public life, and different levels of leadership.

All in all, through preparation, experience, and reflection, we participated through the Asia Leadership Trek in what has become an emerging model for 21st century learning. During research for a forthcoming book on this topic, we interviewed Professor David Garvin from HBS, whose own research, along with that of Professor Srikant M. Datar on the effectiveness of business education, partly led to the creation of the Harvard Business School's innovative FIELD Program. Among other insights, Professor Garvin shared with us a relevant and valuable leadership framework, that of Knowing, Doing, and Being: "First there's 'Knowing,' or gaining knowledge. There are some things you have to know in order to be able to be productive.... The second stage is 'Doing,' or building skills. There are some things you have to know how to do. It's not enough just to possess inert knowledge. You have to have skills...And then the third stage is 'Be-

ing,' or maintaining a sense of identity, responsibility, values, cha-rac-
ter. You need to be able to reflect and think about what you stand
for...and where you draw lines."

Borrowing its structure and rationale, we adapted this framework
of Knowing, Doing, and Being for the Asia Leadership Trek:

Pre-Trek: Learning by 'Knowing'

Regular Course-work	Focused Leadership Program	Country & Working Group	Community Session

Trek: Learning by 'Doing'

Leading workshops in the conference	Giving men-toring sessions and talks on life lessons	History & cultural exposure	Site visits & meetings

Post-Trek: Learning by 'Reflecting'

Book publication	Documentary	Media Publication

What was the outcome for the Trekkers? First, through engagement with government officials, academics, entrepreneurs, journalists, and business leaders, we gained firsthand experience of the
challenges that Asian societies are currently facing in the areas of
education, public leadership, and business innovation. Second, we
learned about the varied practices that each Asian state is currently
implementing in each of these areas. Third, we applied the concepts
and skills we had learned in the classroom by holding workshops

and conferences and adapting them to suit the particular societal and political context of each country. Fourth, we developed essential personal and professional skills in communication, teamwork, and cultural sensitivity through our constant interactions with diverse groups of individuals from all walks of life. Fifth, we extended our own individual research efforts and met a variety of people who helped to mobilize our own leadership initiatives. Lastly, through efforts such as this book, we have been able to reflect on and share our newly gained knowledge and insights.

In each iteration of the Asia Leadership Trek, we plan to learn from our experiences and adapt the program to provide even more meaningful results. We hope that the program will serve as a vehicle for learning innovation in the Harvard, MIT, and Tufts communities, and as the program develops we will not stop at these schools: we believe that we have reached only the tip of the iceberg, and that the Asia Leadership Trek will be the beginning of a great and significant effort in global learning and communication.

Chapter 3

Learning and Service:

An Overview of the Trek's Itinerary, Forums, & Conferences

Hungsoo S. Kim and John Lim, Co-Editors

● ● ●

Asia Leadership Trek 2014

In this chapter we provide an overview of the many meetings, conversations, and tours we engaged in during the Asia Leadership Trek. We also discuss in more detail the two forums and two full-scale conferences that we held in Shanghai, Hong Kong, Kuala Lumpur, and Seoul, respectively. By organizing these events, we sought to impart to our audiences both the cutting-edge theories and leadership training that we had received at Harvard, Tufts, and MIT and the experiences and life lessons of an exceptional group of individuals.

We recognize that such conferences and forums have obvious limitations. We are by no means assuming that we can swoop in and solve all the societal problems of the cities we visited. We also know that it is difficult to influence someone profoundly or measurably build someone's skills within a day. But by engaging people through these events, we seek to act as a starting point for change by exposing them to new perspectives. Even if it is only for a short time, we hope to motivate and challenge them, bringing them outside of their comfort zone. As one of our Trekkers, Saurabh Agarwal from India, put it, "I wish I had been exposed to a program like this when I was growing up to help inspire me and my schoolmates."

Shanghai

Although one city cannot represent all of China, Shanghai is the model that the rest of modern mainland China strives to emulate. Even as recently as ten years ago, one would never have considered China to be a country that contained a budding ecosystem, one capable of supporting world-leading creative talent. Yet we learned about Shanghai's creative scene from dialogues with Mr. Steve Boswell and his colleagues at the Frog Design Company and from young entrepreneurs in China who are developing everything from mobile education apps to concierge and taxi services. It is now well-established that China is a regional or global power in the realm of "hardware," with its massive industrial manufacturing base, but we learned on the Trek that China is rapidly becoming a place where "software" is also created, a place that drives ideas and sets global standards for innovation.

While in Shanghai we also visited the city's future economic engine, its new Free Trade Zone called Nanhui New City, and we gained diverse perspectives of Shanghai's emerging issues from conversations with leaders in media, education, and the non-profit sector.

Thursday, January 2, 2014

6:00am	Bike-Riding through Zhongshan Park
8:00am	Breakfast Dialogue with Rob Schmitz, Shanghai Correspondent for Marketplace; Lenora Chu, Board Member of the Foreign Correspondents Club of Shanghai; and Zixin Li, Founder of Crowd-sourced Social Media Platform "China 30s."
9:00am	Guided Tour of Xinmin Media and Dialogue with Chief Editor, Chen Qiwei
11:00am	Lunch and Networking with Local Entrepreneurs: Haifeng Education, Meiwei, Goocus, Uber China, and Artdore
2:00pm	Guided Tour of Shanghai Free Trade Zone and Briefing by Lingang Group
6:00pm	Guided Tour of the K11 Art Mall

Friday, January 3, 2014

8:00am	Campus Tour and Dialogue with Zheng Fangxian, Principal of High School affiliated to Fudan University
10:00am – 12:00pm	**Asia Leadership Conference 2014 in Shanghai**
10:00am	Opening Remarks by Hungsoo S. Kim, President of the Asia Leadership Trek (ALT)
10:05am	Welcoming Speech by Zheng Fangxian
10:10am	Workshop Breakout Session on '21st Century Competitive Skills, Negotiations and Mediations, Creating Shared Values, Design Thinking and Innovation, and Disciplined Entrepreneurship'
11:30am	Town Hall Meeting on 'What is Leadership' with Teachers and Students moderated by John Lim, Director of International Affairs of ALT

12:00pm	Dialogue with Steve Boswell, General Manager of Frog Design ALT Design Thinking Workshop led by Senior Design Consultants
2:00pm	Dialogue with Christopher Shallis, Environmentalist at The Good Earth Project
4:00pm	Dialogue with Ben Wood, CEO and Head Architect of Shanghai Studio at Xintiandi
6:00pm	Sightseeing at Lujiazie

Youth Leadership Forum

In Shanghai, we held the Youth Leadership Forum at Fudan University on January 3, 2014. Co-organized with the China Young Leaders Foundation and a local student group, Project ConneXion, it featured a panel on leadership as well as mentoring sessions with industry representatives from the fields of business, government, education, and non-profit. Jeff Chen, a visiting undergraduate student from China at Harvard College, moderated the panel on leadership.

One of the many meaningful exchanges during the panel began when a Fudan University student asked, "Is it possible for everyone to be a leader? In China, it seems that only those with a good education and with power can be a leader." The question cut to the heart of one of the many challenges facing China as a developing country with an evident gap between socioeconomic classes. Is it possible to do anything significant in such a country without a prestigious education, money, and connections?

The question was answered by Trekker Roberto Patino, a twenty-six-year-old student from the Harvard Kennedy School who before coming to Harvard assembled a team of 25,000 volunteers for the opposition government in his home country of Venezuela.

He responded, "I think you have a wrong understanding about leadership. A factory worker may not have strong sources of power when he is at the factory, but he still has many opportunities to exercise leadership. He encounters problems in his own network and in society, problems in which he is able to make a difference. He has a family that looks to him for leadership. He may have a village to go back to in the rural area, where he might be expected to create change and solve problems. Leadership is not about being in charge. Many people are in charge but they don't exercise leadership."

Reflecting on this exchange, the Trekkers later explored a bigger question: Can China truly become a world leader in the future? Millions of young Chinese youth are rising to the middle class and from there to positions of influence. We met a few of them at this forum, and they asked curious and frank questions about leadership. Will they have what it takes to lead?

Effective leaders help groups navigate change by showing them how to overcome their toughest challenges. One of China's visionary leaders, Mr. Deng Xiaoping, held the highest position in the country, but the position alone was not what made him a good leader. Rather he gained his reputation as an effective leader by recognizing China's most complex challenges and mobilizing the country's millions of citizens to tackle them together.

If China's youth strive for positions of influence merely for the sake of power, they will not exercise true leadership. But if members of the rising generation in China, no matter their socioeconomic status, follow Mr. Deng's model of recognizing the country's most pressing and complex challenges and mobilizing others to meet those challenges, then China will become a nation of leaders. Not only will they be able to lead China, but also the world.

Hong Kong

Hong Kong is a city populated by people like Global Markets, Mr. Romnesh Lamba, Co-Head of Global Markets at the Hong Kong Stock Exchange. Born in India, he left for the United States to study, and upon landing a job there he changed his citizenship from Indian to American. Years later, finding his way to Hong Kong, he switched from being an American to being a Chinese national. He shared his story with us to show the dynamics of change in the world, one that is Western-oriented but increasingly returning eastward.

The ambiguous nature of identity also characterizes Hong Kong itself, as a special administrative region of China. Though it is a vibrant economic center, it also exists in a state of political limbo. We had the privilege of speaking with President of the Legislative Council (Legco) Jasper Tsang Yok-sing, who told us that the aspiration of people in Hong Kong is to achieve universal suffrage in 2017, when the next Chief Executive is elected. Mr. Tsang, an amiable man who is a former middle-school principal, made the frank admission that he was still uncertain whether or not universal suffrage could be achieved at that time.

Arriving in Hong Kong on a weekend provided us with the enjoyable opportunity of engaging with local university-student ambassadors, who led us on a historical tour of the city. During the following week, along with a visit to Legco, we also visited the Hong Kong Stock Exchange and the HKICC Lee Shau Kee School of Creativity, which demonstrated an inspiring model of education away from public examinations.

Saturday, January 4, 2014

10:00am	Depart for Hong Kong
2:30pm	Central Historical Tour of Hong Kong led by Local University Student Ambassadors
8:00pm	Star Ferry Ride and Sightseeing at Tsim Sha Tsui

Sunday, January 5, 2014

9:00am	Sightseeing of Hong Kong Group 1: Peak Tram, Victoria Peak, Tian Tan Buddha, and Ngong Ping 360 Group 2: Po Lin Monastery, Hong Kong Museum of History, Man Po Temple, and Ten Thousand Buddhas Monastery Group 3: Clock Tower, Tung Choi Street, Wong Tai Sin Street, Ladies Shopping Street, and Mongkok Food Street

Monday, January 6, 2014

7:00am	Breakfast and Conference Briefing by SOW Asia
10:00am	Guided Tour of the Hong Kong Legislative Council (Legco) and Dialogue with Honorable Legco President, Jasper Tsang
1:00pm	Guided Tour of Hong Kong Stock Exchange and Dialogue with Vice President of Global Markets Division, Romnesh Lamba
3:00pm	Campus Tour and Dialogue with Wilson Tse, Principal of Hong Kong International Coaching Community Lee Shau Kee School of Creativity
6:00pm	Networking Event with the Harvard Club of Hong Kong

Tuesday, January 7, 2014

9:00am – 12:30pm	**Asia Leadership Conference 2014 in Hong Kong on 'New Perspectives on Leadership and Social Innovation' at the Hong Kong Polytechnic University**
8:30am	Registration
9:00am	Opening Remarks by Marjorie Yang, GBS, JP, Chairman of Council, the Hong Kong Polytechnic University
9:05am 9:10am	Welcoming Speech by John Lim, Director of International Affairs of ALT Special Talks on 'Doing Good with Business: My Journey from Google to Ashoka' by Jenny Jin (US, MIT MBA)
9:25am	Special Talks on 'Design for Social Innovation' by Alvin Yip, Director of Jockey Club Design Institute for Social Innovation
9:40am	Workshop Breakout Sessions on 'Adaptive Leadership, Building Diverse Leadership Teams, From Good Intentions to Leading Social Change, Exercising Leadership, Innovating NGOs, New Trends in Education and Innovation, Social Responsibilities Through Business, Money, and Society, and Entrepreneurship and Problem Solving'
11:00am	Tea Time and Networking Session
11:20am	Panel Discussions on 'Creating Shared Values' with Sara Minkara (US, HKS MPP), Irene Shao (Canada, HGSE Ed.M.), Paul Yoo (US, HGSE Ed.M.), and Mark Yee (Philippines, HGSE Ed.M.) led by Francis Ngai, Founder and CEO of Social Ventures HK
11:50am	Closing Remarks by Scott Lawson, CEO of SOW Asia, on 'Hong Kong's Social Innovation Ecosystem'

| 12:30pm | Lunch with Social Entrepreneurs |
| 5:00pm | Depart for Singapore |

A Forum on Social Innovation and Multi-sectoral Solutions

In Hong Kong, we co-organized a forum on social innovation with SOW Asia, the Jockey Club Design Institute for Social Innovation (J.C. DISI), and the Institute for Entrepreneurship. The forum, like our conference in Shanghai, was also sponsored by the China Young Leaders Foundation; it was held at the Hong Kong Polytechnic University and included three workshops and five study groups. SOW Asia and J.C. DISI used the event as a platform to gather together about two hundred social entrepreneurs and university students, from a range of different fields, who were interested in social innovation. We learned from Ms. Athena Lam, the program manager at SOW Asia, that the premise for our event directly tackled a common problem in Hong Kong: many young professionals today find themselves in an environment that provides no opportunity for meeting anyone but their immediate industry peers. Individuals interested and engaged in social innovation, like Ms. Lam, are hoping to bridge that gap between different fields by looking for collaborative opportunities across industries.

In our forum, which included diplomats, bankers, teachers, government workers, and development workers, to name only a few, we hoped we could create in miniature an ecosystem in which individuals from different sectors could work together on social innovation. A local Hong Kong university student, who acted as one of our student ambassadors and showed us around the city, told us that he had never met people working in management and finance who were also deeply interested in social initiatives. We hoped through our forum to facilitate similar connections and discoveries.

The complexity of the world today cannot be solved through a singular lens. Hong Kong, like other cities, needs to reinvent itself constantly in order to stay relevant and competitive. But as a financial center with a highly educated population and an ambitious corps of social entrepreneurs, Hong Kong has the potential to be China's model for turning game-changing ideas into sustainable social impact.

Singapore

Singapore is a model of order, a calm change that was palpable after the bustling streets of Hong Kong. The pragmatic, responsible nature of Singaporeans seemed to emanate from everyone, from the academics to the cab drivers. It is this culture of stable pragmatism that has allowed Singapore to thrive.

Yet times are changing in orderly Singapore, as it moves towards a more pluralistic society. The people we met there were not reluctant to voice their opinions. Two academics whom we spoke with at the Lee Kuan Yew School of Public Policy harshly but constructively criticized their government for overlooking essentials in an "economically emancipated" society. Their argument was that although Singapore has been wildly successful economically, the point of such success should be not the success itself but the freedom that success can bring.

How will Singapore move from a hierarchical, authoritative, and conformity-seeking style of governance to one that is more decentralized and pluralistic? That is the big question on the minds of Singaporeans. There is no textbook guide for navigating this transition, nor any examples in history. But when they achieve it—and we have confidence that they will—the transformation will have huge consequences across the region, particularly in China, which looks at Singapore as a model.

During our time in the city we had the chance to speak with several prominent figures, who run Singapore's famously efficient government in the areas of education, tourism, and parks.

Wednesday, January 8, 2014

9:00am	Dialogue with Dr. Tan Oon Seng, Dean of Teacher Education, National Institute of Education
10:30am	Dialogue with Poon Hong Yuen, CEO of NParks & Guided Tour of Singapore Botanic Garden
12:00pm	Lunch at Tiong Bahru Market & Hawker Center
1:00pm	Campus Tour and Dialogue with Chua Chor Huat, Principal of School of Science and Technology
3:00pm	Dialogue with Lawrence Lien, CEO of National Volunteer and Philanthropy Centre, and Chairman and Governor of Lien Foundation
5:00pm	Dinner Hosted by Lawrence Lien at his Residence
8:00pm	Networking Event at the Raffles Hotel

Thursday, January 9, 2014

9:00am	Special Seminars by Donald Low, Associate Dean of the Lee Kuan Yew School of Public Policy, and Yeoh Lam Keong, Senior Research Fellow
10:30am	Dialogue with Lionel Yeoh, Chief Executive of Singapore Tourism Board
12:00pm	Luncheon with Patrick Tay, a Parliament Member of Singapore - Labor Party

1:00pm	Sightseeing of the Marina Bay Sands Hotel
2:00pm	Dialogue with Devadas Krishnadas, Founder of Future Moves
4:00pm	Sightseeing of the Gardens by the Bay
6:00pm	Depart for Kuala Lumpur by Bus

Kuala Lumpur

The problems in Malaysia are many: a racial divide, a middle-income trap, economic inequality, an underperforming education system, and political intractability, among others. On the Trek, however, we found that the country is also blessed with many audacious, reform-minded enthusiasts. While in the country's capital, Kuala Lumpur, we met three of the "10 Inspiring Malaysians" chosen by the media company The Edge: Mr. Azman Mokhtar from Khazanah Nasional, Mr. Wan Saiful Wan Jan from the Institute for Democracy and Economic Affairs (IDEAS), and Dr. Zeti Akhtar Aziz from the Central Bank of Malaysia. One other impressive figure who met with us before we left Kuala Lumpur was Sunway Group Chairman Dr. Jeffrey Cheah.

During our time in Kuala Lumpur we were especially interested to discover the development of an "Asian Leadership Index" at the Iclif Leadership & Governance Centre. The Index identifies a number of attributes and behaviors typical in various Asian countries and offered suggestions on how leaders in those countries might move forward with greater influence and impact. Overall it is a valuable reference and indicates the rising awareness within Asia of the importance of innovative leadership in an age of change.

We were struck by the initiative and leadership demonstrated by the young Malaysians we met, an attitude articulated when we visited the Teach for Malaysia Office: the country's young people are trying different things and asking different questions. We believe that their willingness to experiment with new perspectives and activities will give them the power to lead in the future. We found the people outspoken, constructive, passionate, and full of high hopes for their country, despite the prodigious challenges ahead.

Friday, January 10, 2014

8:00am	Welcoming Breakfast and Guided Tour of the Sunway University and Sunway Group
11:00am	Dialogue with Yayasan Amir, Ahnaz As-Sadat, and Nik Fahme of The Trust School Project
1:00pm	Dialogue with Leaders of Teach for Malaysia (TFM) Panel Discussion on 'Leading Educational Initiatives in a Developing Asian Country' Workshop Breakout Session on 'Adaptive Leadership, Leadership Communications, Public Narrative, and Authentic Leadership' for TFM Fellows
4:00pm	Dialogue with Parliament Members from the Opposition Parties: Tony Pua, Nik Nazmi, and Ong Kian Ming
6:00pm	Dinner with His Royal Highness Dr. Nazrin Shah and Networking with the Harvard Club of Malaysia

Saturday, January 11, 2014

9:30am – 4:00pm	**Asia Leadership Conference 2014 in Kuala Lumpur on 'Malaysia in the 21st Century: Public Leadership, Education and Entrepreneurship'**

9:00am	Registration
9:30am	Opening Remarks by Hungsoo S. Kim, President of ALT
9:35am	Welcoming Speech by Dr. Elizabeth Lee, Senior Executive Director of Sunway Education Group
9:40am	Keynote Speech Tunku Zain Al-'Abidin ibni Tuanku Muhriz, Trustee, Jeffrey Cheah Foundation, and Founding President of Institute for Democracy and Economic Affairs (IDEAS)
10:20am	Tea Break and Networking Session
10:40am	Workshop Breakout Session 1: 'Adaptive Leadership, The 5 Secrets of Powerful Public Speakers, Designing 21st Century Learning Systems, On Mentoring: Navigating Global Careers, Building and Nurturing Diverse Leadership Teams, Leading Social Change, Strategic Impact: Education Entrepreneurship, Design Thinking and Innovation, Competitive Skills and Attributes of the 21st Century Skills, and Effective Decision-Making'
12:00pm	Lunch Break
12:50pm	Leadership Forum with Dr. Zaini Ujang, Secretary General 2 of the Malaysian Education Ministry; Wan Saiful Wan Jan, CEO of IDEAS; and Dr. Ramon Navaratnam, CEO of Asian Strategy and Leadership Institute (ASLI)
2:15pm	Tea Break and Networking Session
2:30pm	Workshop Breakout Session 2: Same Topics
3:45pm	Closing Remarks by Hungsoo S. Kim, President of ALT
6:00pm	Dinner at Kuala Lumpur Tower

Sunday, January 12, 2014

9:00am	Rest Time
12:00pm	Sightseeing of Kuala Lumpur: Merdeka Square, Bukit Bintang, Batu Caves, and National Museum
4:00pm	Tun Abdul Razak Lecture on 'Transforming the Asia Pacific and Turkey' delivered by Honorable Prime Minister of Turkey, Recep Tayyip Erdogan

Monday, January 13, 2014

10:00am	Guided Tour of the KLCC at the Petronas Twin Towers
10:30am	Dialogue with Azman Mokhtar, Managing Director of Khazanah National
12:00pm	Luncheon with Senior Leaders of Khazanah National
2:00pm	Dialogue with Dr. Zeti Akhtar Aziz, Governor of the Central Bank of Malaysia
4:00pm	Dialogue with Kate Sweetman, Director of ICLIF Leadership and Governance Center
6:00pm	Farewell Dinner with Sunway Group Founder and Chairman, Dr. Jeffrey Cheah
11:30pm	Depart for Seoul

A Conference on Leadership in the 21st Century

"Students wanted to learn more about leadership. It was a topic that they thought was relevant but that they didn't know much about, and they wanted solutions to this dilemma." These sentiments from Nikki Skovran, a Trekker from the Harvard Business School, were addressed in our conference in Malaysia, co-organized with Sunway University, the Jeffrey Cheah Foundation, and the UEM Group. With over seven hundred attendees, the conference was a massive undertaking, involving fourteen workshops and seminars running simultaneously. The conference also included a leadership panel with such distinguished individuals as Dr. Zaini Ujang from the Malaysian Ministry of Education, Mr. Wan Saiful Wan Jan from the Institute for Democracy and Economic Affairs (IDEAS), and Dr. Ramon Navaratnam from the Asian Strategy and Leadership Institute (ASLI).

A workshop that particularly struck a chord with the attending students was one on public narrative. Led by Trekkers Daniel Wallance and Zhoulai Zhu, the workshop focused on how to turn values into action. A leader is someone who can instruct, motivate, and mobilize groups by appealing to a shared set of values. The best method for leaders to frame such appeals is to provide their group with a coherent and engaging personal story, but this can be a challenging task for Asians, who come from cultures that encourage more reserve than those in the West and who often find it difficult to express themselves. In this workshop, Daniel and Zhoulai identified the act of storytelling through public narrative as a crucial skill in effective leadership.

One trekker, Kate Bragg from the Harvard Business School, remarked that frameworks such as these helped local students think about leadership in a way that they rarely seemed to come into contact. The ensuing discussion revolved around possible ways in which the use of public narrative could address the problems inflicted on Malaysian society by race-based politics. If leaders in the country possessed the skill of public narrative, one student opined, then a lot of the nation's divisiveness could be overcome. A new culture of communication could spring up between ethnicities, cultures, and generations. The discussion reminded us that, although it is impossible to provide readymade solutions for another country's problems in one day-long conference, the learning experiences and conversations that arise during the conference could very well lead one day to solutions.

Seoul

Why is South Korea "abnormal"? As explained by Dr. Hahm Chaibong from The Asan Institute for Policy Studies, the adjective is appropriate because South Korea lives in a paradox: it has become one of the most vibrant regions in the world while being threatened on all sides by historical and military tension. Though it signed a ceasefire agreement in 1953, South Korea is still technically at war with the North and is under constant threat of being turned into a "sea of fire." Only hours from Seoul, the Demilitarized Zone (DMZ), which we visited on the Trek, was a reminder of this threat. Despite its name, the DMZ is the most militarized area in the world. Yet, despite this looming danger, South Korea has successfully moved from being a wartorn nation and one of the poorest economies in the world to being the thirteenth largest economy on the planet.

Our sobering visit to the DMZ and our conversations with North Korean defectors from the North Korea Strategy Group were contrasted with a visit to glitzy Gangnam, a meeting in a fancy Citibank boardroom, a tour of the futuristic Samsung product showroom, test-drives of yet-to-be-released Hyundai luxury cars, and the glamour of the CJ Entertainment's K-pop show. Though a few members of the Trek, including the authors of this chapter, had lived in Seoul at various times in their lives, our visit to the city was a vivid reminder of how far South Korea has come.

Tuesday, January 14, 2014

10:00am	Guided Tour of the Incheon International Airport (IIA) Dialogue with Jung Chang-soo, President of IIA on 'What is Behind IIA's Success as the World's Best Airport for 7 Consecutive Years?
2:00pm	Special Seminar by Dr. Hahm Chaibong, President of Asan Institute for Policy Studies on 'Modern History of Korea and the 21st Century Northeast Asia Geopolitics'
4:00pm	Guided Tour of the Blue House Special Seminar on 'Creating a Viable Ecosystem for Entrepreneurship and Innovation in Korea' by Dr. Yoon Chang-bun, Senior Presidential Secretary for Future Strategy
8:00pm	Nanta Show – Korean Non-verbal Comedy Show

Wednesday, January 15, 2014

10:00am	Dialogue with Hwang Woo-yeo, Spokesperson of Saenuri Party, and Chung Mong-joon, a National Assemblyman of Saenuri Party
12:00pm	Luncheon with Kil Jeong-woo, a National Assemblyman of Saenuri Party
3:00pm	Sightseeing of the Gangnam District
5:00pm	Guided Tour of the Samsung Innovation Center
6:30pm	North Korea Strategy Group
7:00pm	Dialogue with North Korean Refugees through the North Korea Strategy Group
8:00pm	Jump! Comic Martial Arts Performance

Thursday, January 16, 2014

8:00am	Guided Tour of the Demilitarized Zone (DMZ): UNCMAC Brief, Tour of Panmunjom, Op Dora and Tunnel 3
4:00pm	Corporate Tour & Sponsored Shopping Dialogue with Senior Leaders of Amore Pacific
6:30pm	Corporate Tour and Dialogue with Senior Leaders of CJ Entertainment Live K-pop Concert Show 'Mnet Countdown'

Friday, January 17, 2014

10:00am	Dialogue with Ha Young-koo, Chairman of Citibank Korea
1:30pm	Guided Tour & Presentation by the Hyundai Motors Future Research and Development Center Test Driving of a New Premium Model, Genesis, Electronic and Hydrogen-fueled Cars
5:00pm	Dialogue with Senior Leaders of Kim & Chang. Special Seminar on 'South Korea and the Geopolitics of the Northeast Asia in the 21st Century' by Dr. Park Jin, Senior Advisor of Kim & Chang. Networking Reception with Attorneys at Kim & Chang

Saturday, January 18, 2014

9:30am – 4:30pm	**Asia Leadership Conference 2014 in Seoul on 'Social Innovation and Impact'**
9:00am	Registration
9:30am	Opening Remarks by Hungsoo S. Kim, President of ALT
9:40am	Keynote Speech by Dr. Kil Jeong-woo on 'New Leadership Needed in the 21st Century Korea'

10:00am	Tea Break and Networking Session
10:20am	Workshop Breakout Session 1: 'Adaptive Leadership, The 5 Secrets of Powerful Public Speakers, Designing 21st Century Learning Systems, On Mentoring: Navigating Global Careers, Building and Nurturing Diverse Leadership Teams, Leading Social Change, Strategic Impact: Education Entrepreneurship, Design Thinking and Innovation, Competitive Skills and Attributes of the 21st Century Skills, and Effective Decision-Making'
11:40am	Lunch Break
12:30pm	Special Talks by Margaret McKenzie (US, Fletcher MALD), Fabian Toegel (Germany, HKS MPA), and Cara Repasky (USA, HBS MBA)
1:40pm	Tea Break and Networking Session
2:00pm	Workshop Breakout Session 2: Same Topics
3:20pm	Professional Skills Development Seminars
4:20pm	Closing Remarks by Hungsoo S. Kim, President of ALT
5:00pm	Sightseeing of Seoul: Gwanghwamun, Myundong, and Insadong
6:00pm	Farewell Dinner

The Expectations of Leaders

April Bang, an instructor at Yonsei University in Seoul, led a panel of distinguished speakers in our conference on social innovation held at the university. The conference's other keynote speakers included Gil Alterovitz, a Harvard Medical School professor who spoke on "Education and Entrepreneurship in Asia: Leadership in the 21st Century," and Korea Assemblyman Kil Jeong-woo, who spoke on

"21st Century Leadership in Korea."

A former teacher's assistant to Professor Ronald Heifetz at the Harvard Kennedy School, April Bang now teaches a course on exercising leadership. Employing Professor Heifetz's framework of adaptive leadership and the case-in-point method, an experiential learning pedagogy that uses the class experience itself as a case to be analyzed, her course has already gained recognition as one of the most impactful at Yonsei University. Professor Heifetz's own course was named the "Most Influential Class" in a 2013 poll of alumni conducted by SLATE (Strengthening Learning and Teaching Excellence), the teaching and learning center at the Harvard Kennedy School.

"Leadership is dangerous," Bang boldly stated in her talk during the Trek conference. Her message on leadership was wholly relevant to Korea's current position. She shared a personal narrative about making hard decisions and causing loss, and the message resonated with many of the initiatives that South Korea is currently pursuing, such as the development of a creative economy and the possible unification with North Korea. For individuals who decide to take on the mantle of the country's leadership, the future in Korea will be difficult. Success for these leaders will depend on changing established hierarchies and challenging the status quo, whether they are leading in the business, government, or non-profit sectors. They will have to take actions that may cause people loss.

During the many discussions at the conference, we observed that the perspective on leadership of many Korean young people was similar to what we had seen in Shanghai: they believed that being a leader simply meant having authority. This dry and rigid vision of leadership is currently predominant in Korea, but if the country is to succeed in conquering its pressing challenges, its leaders—like those of all the other countries we visited—will need to embark on a more "dangerous," innovative, and dynamic form of leadership, one capable of embracing many different perspectives and visions for the future.

Asia Leadership Trek III

After the success of our first ever January Trek, we had to plan for the next Asia Leadership Trek (ALT), which was scheduled six months later, in June 2016. Looking at a Google map of the entire continent of Asia, we bounced ideas back and forth about where we should travel this time. Already we had forty-four soon-to-be Trekkers, representing twenty-four countries and bringing varying areas of interest—security, environmental sustainability, human rights, startups, governance, regulations. When I met with them, I could feel how thrilled they were about the prospect of exploring countries and places they had heard of but never visited. As organizers, we did not have an easy task in developing an underlying theme for the upcoming ALT. Though we soon chose the destinations, we had a challenging time connecting the dots between the destinations and establishing the order of the journey. Over and over we asked ourselves, "What do we want to be the main takeaways for Trekkers this time?" and "How does every country or city that we visit relate to each other?"

Before us were Seoul, Beijing, and Tokyo in Northeast Asia and Yangon, Jakarta, and Bangkok in Southeast Asia. We chose two different regions because we wanted to gain a better understanding of both places: in the Northeast, we hoped to explore the complex regional dynamics that operate among Korea, China, and Japan; in the Southeast, we hoped to investigate the differences, both conspicuous and subtle, among the ten countries in the region, which have nonetheless come together under one umbrella of shared interests. Going to both regions would allow us to see strikingly different inter-country relationships at work.

We also aimed to show our Trekkers several different levels of social and economic development, from the most advanced to the least developed. We wanted them to witness what leaders in the former have done to bring their societies out of poverty and conflict, and to observe what leaders in the latter are doing today to overcome similar challenges. In this endeavor, we wanted the Trekkers to see for themselves the concerns that arise at different levels of socioeconomic development, including environmental degradation, changes in mentality and culture, and uncertainty about the future.

Eventually we chose to travel from the northern to the southern regions of Asia. Not only did we want our Trekkers to observe how diverse and colorful Asia is, dispelling any misconceptions that every part of Asia is the same, we also hoped that they would appreciate its innumerable variations in culture and history. Many communities in Asia's diverse nations share things in common, such as filial piety, hierarchical dynamics, strong family values, and a positive attitude toward education, but they differ on many issues too, including race, language, culture, and even ways of doing businesses. In addition, we wanted the Trekkers to learn about the influence of religion, politics, and geography in each country.

While focusing on these differences, the Trek would also emphasize shared larger themes in the places we visited. The Trekkers, we hoped, would notice that many Asian countries have gone through or are currently undergoing rapid economic and social growth. We would give them a chance to examine these changes in depth, analyzing Asia's deeper integration into the global marketplace and the effects of international politics on diverse cultures and ways of thinking.

Northeast Asia

With close economic ties and cultural activities tying the three countries together, millions of tourists and students cross the borders of Japan, Korea, and China each year. Yet tensions over the past and territorial conflicts are holding these three countries back, preventing them from uniting to seek a vibrant and promising future together.

While Korea and Japan share the fundamental values of a democratic rule of law and a market economy, they clash over the territorial dispute concerning the sovereignty of Dokdo/Takeshima and the content of Japanese textbooks—including the topics of "comfort women," forced labor, and other brutalities committed during the Japanese occupation. These controversial subjects still haunt the relationship between the two countries, despite their similar political and economic systems.

China and Korea are currently enjoying an unprecedented level of economic connection, yet concerns about the political dynamics surrounding North Korea, along with pending territorial conflicts over a small island near the coast of Korea, are keeping them from fully realizing a collaborative partnership.

Tensions are strongest in China-Japan relations. These two countries have close economic and social ties, but they also face deep layers of long-standing, unresolved conflict, ranging from war crimes during the colonial era to territorial disputes over Senkaku/Diaoyu Island and the South China Sea.

One news article in 2013 noted that a majority of citizens in each of the three countries view the others unfavorably. The distrust has been paralleled by significant downturns in trades and investments, in some cases by double digits. During the Trek, we investigated what political, economic, and social leaders in these three nations thought about the recent developments and sought their ideas on how the trio might improve their relations so as to make progress in the future.

Tokyo

We visited Japan first because we wanted to hear their views on the claims made by the other two countries. We also wanted to discover how a mature economy like Japan viewed its past, present, and future. Not only we were keen to know more about its relationships with the countries under its influence, we hoped to learn about the best practices that had helped Japan rise from the ashes of World War II to its current status as a global powerhouse. With a mature economy and an established democracy, Japan is a model for developing nations in Asia. Yet it has a rapidly aging population, an extremely low birth rate, and limited female labor-force participation. We wanted to find out how Japanese leaders were dealing with issues that no other Asian nations are currently facing.

Thursday, June 5, 2014

9:00am	Dialogue with Senior Leaders of NHK
11:00am	Presentation & Tour of the Meiji Jingu Shrine
2:30pm	Guided Tour of the National Diet
3:30pm	Dialogue with 12 HKS-Graduated Parliament Members of the Liberal Democratic Party
5:30pm	Dialogue with Senior Leaders of the Japan International Cooperation Agency (JICA)
6:30pm	Welcoming Reception by JICA and Harvard Club of Japan with a Presence of Former UN High Commissioner for Refugees (UNHCR) and Chairman of the UNICEF Executive Board, Sadako Ogata

Friday, June 6, 2014

9:00am	Tour of Asakusa Sensoji Temple & Nakamise
11:00am	Presentation and Dialogue with 14 Senior Executives of Mitsubishi Corporation
12:00pm	Luncheon with Senior Leaders of the Mitsubishi Corporation
2:00pm	Dialogue with Toshihiko Fukui, President (Former Governor of the Bank of Japan); Akinari Horii, Director of International Affairs; and Kunihiko Miyake, Research Director of Canon Institute of Global Studies
4:00pm	Presentation and Dialogue with 8 Senior Executives of Toyota Motors
5:00pm	Guided Tour of Mega Web of Toyota Motors
7:00pm	Leadership Mentoring Session with High School Students of Route H, Benesse Group

Saturday, June 7, 2014

4:00am	Tsukiji Fish Market Tour
9:00am – 1:00pm	**Asia Leadership Conference 2014 in Tokyo co-organized with Impact Japan, World Economic Forum Global Shapers of Japan, and TEDx Todai**
9:30am	Welcoming Speech by Hungsoo S. Kim, President of ALT
9:35am	Special Talks by Saleh Machnouk (Lebanon, HKS MCMPA), Dafu Zhang (China, MIT MBA), Juan Remolina (Colombia, HKS MPA), and Shazia Khan (US/Pakistan, HGSE Ed.M.)
10:30am	Tea Break
10:45am	Workshop Breakout Session 1 on 'Adaptive Leadership, Leadership Communications, Leading Social Change, Design Thinking and Innovation, and Effective Decision-Making'
12:00pm	Team Building Exercise
12:30pm	Closing Remarks by Jiro Yoshino, Japan Director of ALT
12:35pm	Group Photo
12:40pm	Networking Event
2:00pm	Tour of Tokyo in Small Groups Group 1: Akhibara Group 2: Shibuya & Shinjuku Group 3: Odaiba & Ginza Group 4: Roppongi Hills & Asakusa
6:00pm	Farewell Party at Old Man's Un Shiodome

Seoul

In Korea, the major themes we pursued were the tensions between North and South Korea; South Korea's economic transformation, from its humble beginnings in the 1950s to its modern-day prosperity, thanks to a determined pursuit of international markets and the government's encouragement of innovation; and, lastly, the government's promotion of education to enhance the country's industrial and economic competitiveness in the global market. Today, Korea maintains a stable economic growth and stands tall on the world arena, despite being surrounded by other superpowers, such as China and the U.S. The country's soft power has been expanding through the appeal of its popular culture (Korean Wave, or Hallyu) worldwide. Yet, despite the country's internationally popular TV shows, music hits, and beauty products, Korea seems to have the smallest influence on the rising animosities in the Northeast region.

Sunday, June 8, 2014

6:00am	Depart for Seoul
3:00pm	Tour of the Seoul Royal Palace, Gyeongbokgung
6:00pm	Welcoming Dinner at Insadong
8:00pm	Group Time at Hongdae

Monday, June 9, 2014

8:00am	To Samsung Electronics Headquarters in Suwon
10:00am	Presentation by David Eun, Vice President of Samsung Electronics, on (a) Samsung's Survival Strategy, (b) The Trends of the Software and Quality Care Development, and (c) Samsung's New Initiatives in Promoting Entrepreneurships & Supporting Start-ups
10:45am	Presentation by Dr. Jaeyoon Kim, Executive Director of Samsung Economic Research Institute, on (a) Samsung's Survival Strategy, and (b) Challenges and Opportunities
11:30am	Guided Tour of the Samsung Innovation Museum
12:30pm	Lunch hosted by David Eun, Vice President of Samsung Electronics
1:30pm	To Seoul
3:00pm	Tour of Seoul in Small Groups Group 1: War Museum & Public Bath at Yongsan Dragon Group 2: Seoul Tower & Myungdong
	Group 3: Namdaemun & Dongdamum Fashion Shopping Group 4: Gangnam & Apgujeong

Tuesday, June 10, 2014

9:15am	Dialogue with the Honorable Speaker of the National Assembly, Chung Ui-hwa
10:00am	Guided Tour of the National Assembly
2:30pm	Corporate Tour & Sponsored Shopping Dialogue with Senior Leaders of Amore Pacific
4:00pm	Meeting with Kim & Chang Special Seminar on 'The Role of Korea in Asia and the World' by Dr. Park Jin, Senior Advisor at Kim & Chang Special Talks by Miguel Santos (Venezuela/Spain, HKS MCMPA) on 'Political Reform Measures in Venezuela' and Gal Shimon Levy (Israel, HKS MPP) on 'The Start-up Nation: Israel' Networking Reception with Attorneys at Kim & Chang

| 8:00pm | JUMP Show – Korean Martial Arts Comedy Show |

Wednesday, June 11, 2014

10:00am	Dialogue with Citizens' Alliance for North Korea Human Rights & Testimony by a North Korean Refugee
1:00pm	Guided Tour of the Demilitarized Zone (DMZ): UNCMAC Brief, Tour of Panmunjom, Op Dora and Tunnel 3
5:50pm	Departure for Beijing, China

Beijing

While on the Trek, one of the key questions we hoped to answer was how other capitals across Asia are responding to the economic ascent of China. Countries throughout the region are becoming increasingly dependent on China for their economic prosperity, but they are simultaneously apprehensive of China's growing military power, a concern fueled by uncertainties about how China will exercise its power in the future. Asian nations like Korea, Thailand, and— to some extent—Indonesia rely on the U.S. for security, and China's growing military power thus poses a special threat for these countries, since they may be forced to choose sides in the event of a military confrontation between the U.S. and China. Even if there is no armed conflict, many elites in these smaller countries worry that China will use its economic power as political leverage. Given these fears, we wanted to hear from Chinese leaders how they viewed their country's rise in the region and how they planned to win the hearts of wary leaders in neighboring countries.

Thursday, June 12, 2014

9:30am	Dialogue with Chinese Entrepreneurs at the Garage Cafe, Start-up Incubator and Accelerator Hub
12:30pm	Dialogue with Senior Policy Strategists at the Chinese Academy for Social Sciences: Dr. Zhang Yunling, Director of International Studies, and Dr. Yang Danzhi, Assistant Director of the Center for Regional Security Studies
3:00pm	Meeting with the Hillhouse Capital and Academy hosted by Lei Zhang, Chairman of the Hillhouse Group
7:30pm	Harvard, MIT, and Tufts Fletcher Alumni Networking Event

Friday, June 13, 2014

10:00am	Dialogue with Gao Xiqing, Vice-Chairman and President, and Cao Yu, Managing Director of Board of Directors of China Investment Corporation
2:00pm	Guided Tour of the Lenovo Corporation Dialogue with Liu Xiaolin, Vice President of Strategy & Marketing of Lenovo Group
4:00pm	Guided Tour of the Forbidden City and Tiananmen Square
7:00pm	Dinner hosted by Allen Liang, HKS Alumnus and President of Directors of Sany Foundation

Saturday, June 14, 2014

9:00am – 5:00pm	**Asia Leadership Conference 2014 in Beijing at Renmin University**
9:00am	Registration
9:20am	Opening Remarks by Hungsoo S. Kim, President of ALT
9:25pm	Welcoming Speech by Peter Bai, Head of China Young Leaders Foundation

9:30am	Keynote Speech 1: 'Chinese Interpretation of Leadership' by Dr. Zeng Minhua, Professor at Renmin University
9:50am	Keynote Speech 2: 'Leadership in China in the 21t Century' by Audrene Eliot (France, HKS MCMPA)
10:10am	Tea Break & Networking Session
10:30am	Special Talks 1: 'Empowerment for Leadership in the 21st Century: New Challenges for Organizing Universities' by Christian Brei (Germany, HKS MPA)
10:50am	Special Talks 2: 'Lessons in My Leadership Journey' by Mitchell Ji (US, HBS MBA)
11:10am	Panel Discussion on 'Perspective Leadership: What and How' by Valeri von der Tann (Germany, HKS MPP), John Lim (Philippines, Fletcher MALD), Andi Sparringa (Indonesia, Fletcher MALD), Karly Schledwitz (US, HKS MPP), and Juan Remolina (Colombia, HKS MPA), followed by Q&A Session
12:00pm	Lunch
1:00pm	Workshop Breakout Session 1: Leadership for Organizational Renewal, Authentic Leadership, Leadership Communications, Leadership Through Storytelling, Introduction to Negotiations, Disciplined Entrepreneurship, and Building a Creative Confidence
2:20pm	Tea Break and Networking Session
2:40pm	Workshop Breakout Session 2: Same Topics
4:00pm	Closing Remarks by Hungsoo S. Kim, President of ALT
4:10pm	Networking Reception
6:00pm	Chinese Cultural Night involving a Traditional Dance, Martial Arts Performance, Painting, Writing, and Crafts

Sunday, June 15, 2014

9:00am	Dialogue with Dr. Xu Hongcai, CCTV Commentator and Professor at Renmin University
10:30am	Networking Event with Faculties and Students of Renmin University
1:30pm	Tour of the Great Wall

Monday, June 16, 2014

9:00am	Campus Tour and Dialogue with Dr. David Li, Dean, and Julian Chang, Associate Dean of Schwartzman Scholars, Tsinghua University
11:00am	Tour of Temple of Heaven and Yonghe Temple
2:30pm	Guided Tour of China Center for International Economic Exchange, and Dialogue with Dr. Huang Yiping, Professor at the National Schools of Development, Peking University
7:30pm	Departure for Yangon, Myanmar

Southeast Asia

Southeast Asia consists of ten countries that are closely connected by the Association of Southeast Asian Nations (ASEAN). The ASEAN Economic Community (AEC) brings these countries even closer together. In 2014, the AEC was the third biggest economy in Asia and the seventh largest in the world. All told, the ASEAN population comprises approximately 625 million people. It has a huge and growing young population that represents extensive opportunities for innovation and economic growth. We chose to explore this part of Asia because it is dynamic and offers so much potential.

Yangon

Myanmar has recently undergone historic changes toward development and democracy. Though it was once a great nation, catastrophic governance led to its becoming one of the poorest states in the region. Now, however, the country is opening up to the world again and moving toward democracy, led by Madame Aung San Suu Kyi, after the military's decision to renounce its power after decades of authoritarian rule. With a wealth of natural resources, Myanmar has huge economic potential and seems to be set on a path to a prosperous future.

Tuesday, June 17, 2014

9:00am	Dialogue with Aung Min, Director of Myanmar Peace Center and Myanmar President's Office Minister, Dr. Min Zaw Oo, Academic Director of Myanmar Peace Center, and Khin Ye, Myanmar Home Affairs Minister
11:00am	Dialogue with Jim Taylor, Co-Founder and Chief Executive, and Debbie Aung Din, Co-Founder of Proximity Designs
1:00pm	Lunch hosted by Dr. Lam Kin Chung, Chairman of LKC Morning Sun Charity Fund and Zhong Yang Group Holdings, Hong Kong
2:30pm	Tour & Shopping at Bogyoke Aung San Market
4:00pm	Dialogue with Derek Mitchell, US Ambassador to Myanmar, and State Department's State Alumni Young Leaders
5:30pm	Tour of Shwedagon Pagoda
7:30pm	Dinner Hosted by Project Hub Yangon Special Talks by Thomas Galloway (US, Fletcher MALD) and Thomas Favennec (France, HKS MPA)

Wednesday, June 18, 2014

11:00am	Dialogue with Dr. Thein Lwin, Education Committee Chair, and Senior Leaders, of the Myanmar Opposition Party, National League for Democracy (NLD)
12:30pm	Dialogue with Paradorn Kunkongkaphan, Managing Director of MK Group of Companies, Kyaw Myo Htut, Former Myanmar's Ambassador to the US, Than Lwin, Deputy Chairman of Kanbawza Bank, Dr. Thant Myint U, President of Yangon Heritage Trust, and U Kyaw Kyaw Maung, Governor of Central Bank of Myanmar
2:00pm	Lunch Hosted by MK Group of Companies
4:30pm	Dialogue with U Myint Swe, Chief Minister of Yangon Region, U Win Aung, Chairman, and Senior Leaders of the Union of Myanmar Federation of Chambers of Commerce (UMFCCI)
5:50pm	Departure for Bangkok, Thailand

Bangkok

Thailand is a constitutional monarchy with a revered king who has an undeniable influence on the nation. It is the world's most heavily Buddhist country and has never been colonized. Once, it served as a role model for economic and social development to many other countries in the region. Unfortunately, it has recently lost its way due to several political coups. Nor has Thailand been able to adopt a fully functioning democratic system of governance. Today, the country's dynamism has faded and no longer stands out, but it still remains one of the top holiday destinations in the region, attracting tourists from all over the world. It has weathered economic setbacks and political turmoil in the past, and it remains optimistic about its long-term prospects.

Thursday, June 19, 2014

9:00am	Guided Tour of the United Nations Economic and Social Commission for Asia and the Pacific (UNESCAP)
10:00am	Dialogue with Senior Officials of the UNESCAP
1:30pm	Dialogue with Kristie Kenney, US Ambassador to Thailand
4:30pm	Dialogue with Pichai Chuensuksawasdi, Editor-in-Chief of Bangkok Post
7:00pm	Corporate Presentation on the 'State of Thai Private Sector,' and Dialogue with Kevin Whitcraft, CEO of RMA Group
9:00pm	Networking Reception with Harvard Club of Thailand Hosted by RMA Group

Friday, June 20, 2014

9:00am	Dialogue with Dr. Somkiat Tangkitvanit, President, and Senior Leaders of the Thailand Development Research Institute (TDRI) on 'Educational Reforms to Overcome Thailand's Middle-Income Trap'
12:00pm	Luncheon with Senior Leaders of the Stock Exchange of Thailand (SET)
1:00pm	Dialogue with Dr. Sathit Limpongpan, Chairman of SET
4:00pm	Dialogue with M.R Pridiyathorn Devakula, Former Deputy Prime Minister, Finance Minister and Economic Advisor to the National Council of Peace and Order, and Dr. Veerathai Santiprabhob, Chief Strategy Officer of SET
6:00pm	Dialogue with Abhisit Vejjajiva, Honorable Former Prime Minister of Thailand and Leader of the Democrat Party; Chuti Krairiksh, Secretary General of the Democrat Party; and Korn Chatikavanij, Former Information and Communication Technology Minister, and Finance Minister
7:00pm	Dinner hosted by the Democrat Party

Saturday, June 21, 2014

9:00am – 12:30pm	**Community Service Exercise** **- Group 1: Bangkok Slum Reality Tour organized by LocalAlike.com** **- Group 2: Asia Leadership Conference 2014 in Bangkok at Teach for Thailand (TFT)**
9:00am	Opening Remarks by Hungsoo S. Kim, President of ALT
9:10am	TFT Introduction by Vichitapol Pholpoke, CEO & Founder of TFT
9:20am	Workshop Breakout Session 1 on 'Competitive Skills of the 21st Century, Developing Metacognition Skills, Design Thinking & Innovation, and Adaptive Leadership'
10:40am	Tea Break & Networking Session
11:00am	Workshop Breakout Session 2: Same Topics
12:20pm	Closing Remarks by Fuadi Pitsuwan (Thailand, HKS MPA), Thailand Director of ALT
12:30pm	Networking Session
2:00pm	Free Time Group 1: Thai Massage Group 2: Street Shopping
6:00pm	Muay Thai Show

Sunday, June 22, 2014

9:00am	Group Tour of Bangkok: (a) Gold Buddha Temple, (b) Royal Grand Palace, (c) Temple of the Emerald Buddha, (d) Boat Tour on Chao Praya River, and (e) Wat Po, Temple of the Reclining Buddha
5:00pm	Dinner at Thailand's Best Pad Thai Restaurant, Thipsamai Pad Thai
8:55pm	Depart for Jakarta, Indonesia

Jakarta and Bali

Indonesia is the world's most populous Muslim nation. A vast archipelago of some 17,000 islands, with a population of 250 million people from diverse backgrounds, Indonesia views tourism and the creative economy—meaning those industries that take human resources and knowledge for their main input—as the best way of increasing its economic productivity. The links between education, leadership, and economic success are vital. After decades of military-backed government, Indonesia has now become a role model for peaceful and democratic transfers of power in Southeast Asia. While on the Trek, we were eager to learn how the world's fourth most populous nation, with more than 300 different ethnic groups, was responding to the challenges and opportunities of its huge consumer economy, while promoting peace and prosperity according to its official motto: "Bhinneka Tunggal Ika," or "Unity in Diversity."

Monday, June 23, 2014

1:00pm	Corporate Presentation & Dialogue with Putri Kuswisnuwardhani, CEO of Mustika Ratu, and Miss Indonesia
2:00pm	Spa Session Sponsored by Mustika Ratu
4:00pm	Corporate Presentation by Metro TV
5:00pm	Leadership Communications Workshop at Metro TV for 40 Mid-Level Managers
7:00pm	Welcome Dinner

Tuesday, June 24, 2014

10:00am	Courtesy Call on His Excellency Susilo Bambang Yudhoyono, President of the Republic of Indonesia, and 12 Cabinet Ministers
12:00pm	Guided Tour of the Presidential Palace, Merdeka
1:00pm	Dialogue with Daniel Sparringa, Senior Advisor to the President of Republic of Indonesia for Political Communications
3:00pm	Dialogue with Honorable Minister of Tourism, Culture and Creative Economy, Mari Elka Pangestu
6:00pm	Networking Reception and Dinner with the Indonesian Young Entrepreneurs Association

Wednesday, June 25, 2014

10:00am	Dialogue with Honorable Minister of Foreign Affairs, Marty Natalegawa
11:30am	Guided Tour of the Foreign Ministry
12:00pm	Lunch Hosted by the Foreign Ministry
1:00pm – 6:00pm	**Asia Leadership Conference 2014 in Jakarta at the Indonesian Foreign Ministry**
1:00pm	Opening Remarks by Hungsoo S. Kim, President of ALT
1:10pm	Forum Talk on 'Attributes of the 21st Century Leadership' with Juan Remolina (Colombia, HKS MPA), Fuadi Pitsuwan (Thailand, HKS MPP), Antara Lahiri (India, HKS MPA), Erica Leinmiller (USA,
2:10pm	HKS MPP), and Jieun Baek (USA, HKS MPP)
2:30pm	Tea Break and Networking Session
	Workshop Breakout Session 1 on 'Competitive Skills of the 21st Century, Developing Metacognition Skills, Design Thinking & Innovation, Leadership Communications, and Adaptive Leadership'

3:50pm	Tea Break and Networking Session
4:10pm	Workshop Breakout Session 2: Same Topics
5:30pm	Closing Remarks by Andi Sparringa (Indonesia, Fletcher MALD), Indonesia Director of ALT, and a Foreign Service Officer at the Indonesian Foreign Ministry
7:30pm	Dialogue with John Riady, Director of the Lippo Group
9:30pm	ALT Farewell Dinner at Senayan City

Thursday, June 26, 2014

11:30am	Dialogue with Soetikno Soedarjo, CEO of MRA Group
2:00pm	Tour of Jakarta: National Monument, Istiqlal Mosque, Jakarta History Museum, and Merdeka Square
6:00pm	Meeting with Senior Leaders at AirAsia Indonesia
8:00pm	Departure for Boston or an Optional Trek to Bali

We put this book together because we wanted to give those who haven't yet gone on an Asia Leadership Trek the opportunity to experience Asia as we did—through on-the-ground observations, direct insights from current leaders in the region, and interactions with the next generation of leaders in business, government, and social enterprise.

Happy reading!

Part 2

:

New Perspectives

| Chapter 4 |

Shanghai:
A City of Two Worlds

Zhoulai Zhu

Ed.M., Harvard Graduate School of Education

● ● ●

The moment I set foot on the ground at Pudong International Airport, I feel alive, regardless of the grueling seventeen-hour flight from the other side of the world. I am back in Shanghai, a city that embraces my wonder, excites my palate, and fascinates me with its unique blend of East and West. Half a year's study at Harvard University has not lessened my love for the city, and immediately I am struck with a yearning for lip-smacking Xiaoyang dumplings. I stride along the sidewalk through the crowds, with the soft, light, endearing Shanghai dialect flowing through my ears.

Coming from a linguistics and education background, I am inclined to know people from their language, with a belief that language carries more than the message of the words themselves. The smoldering tension between English and Chinese language education in Shanghai reveals to me the city's dilemma between two identities. Despite the recent trend in the city of children starting to learn English at a younger age, the general opinion is that too much English colors kids' minds and blurs their Chinese identity, since language inevitably transmits values and culture. Such debates have gradually spread out nationwide, culminating in a motion by a deputy of the National People's Congress to cancel English classes before secondary school. Though the motion ended up becoming a joke ridiculed by Shanghainese, it got me thinking about how Shanghai is living its "double identity."

My arrival in Shanghai coincides nicely with the arrival of the year 2014. Irene Shao, a fellow trekker from Canada, invites me and other early birds from the Trek to a rooftop party on New Year's Eve, during which we can look out over half the city, including the Bund, where all the skyscrapers stand as the city's pride. The countdown entertainment has filled the Bund with tens of thousands of people who have managed to keep a foothold in the over-crowded place, celebrating their own growth along with the city's prosperity. We too kick off our party against the dazzling sparkly fireworks. Watching the spire of the Jin Mao Building from afar, I am suddenly caught by a distinct sense of déjàvu. One summer night on the top of Rockefeller Center, I shouted to my friends, "Hey, that's like the Jin Mao Building in Shanghai!" Now here I am, back in a bigger version of New York, its expansion still marching on.

But if I have learned one thing about cultural identity over my last six months in Cambridge, Massachusetts, it is this: putting on a comfy Old Navy t-shirt and Levi's jeans does not change who I am. True, I understand more about Western mindsets and behaviors after living in the U.S., but has the collision of disparate ideas altered my fundamental perspective? Hardly. Beneath Shanghai's futuristic façade of steel and glass, Confucianism runs deep, and it is a philosophy far removed from Western traditions. It is striking how differently Easterners and Westerners think, and the contrast is reflected in one of our first meetings with Xinmin Media, China's biggest media company.

Collectivism vs. Individualism

Seated in the middle of an ornate conference room, Mr. Chen Qiwei extends a warm welcome to all the Trekkers. He is the Chief Editor of *Xinmin Evening News*, one of the three major Chineselanguage newspapers in the city. Sitting across from him, Mr. John Lim, our Trek leader, offers a brief introduction of the members of the Asia Leadership Trek and its mission. Then, to my surprise, he asks a bold question about how Mr. Chen perceives the relationship between government and journalists, and how he strikes a balance between government censorship and journalistic freedom. Though John puts it very nicely, the question unsettles my Chinese nerves. I assumed that such questions would eventually come up at some point, but I never expected that John would drop the bomb so quickly. While the editors from Xinmin Media frown at Mr.Lim's question with thinly veiled astonishment, the rest of the Trekkers seem more curious than surprised. As the interpreter, I stumble over the words, trying to approach the question more tactfully. Will it put an end to the convivial atmosphere? I hold my breath.

My worries, however, turn out to be unnecessary. Mr. Chen, still wearing a friendly smile, assures us that ample freedom is granted to all his journalists for their daily work. But he argues that absolute freedom does not exist in any part of the world. We ask how he decides whether or not a piece of news should be published. He claims he will approve any articles as long as "they are good for the whole society," which Mr. Chen holds to be the social responsibility of all journalists. It sounds perfectly reasonable to a Chinese ear, except that "good for the society" might need more explanation. I am relieved that we have not caused an unpleasant scene, even if some Trekkers may not buy Mr. Chen's standard.

Later on the bus, one of the Trekkers sneers at what we have heard. Born and raised in America, he is convinced that journalists' responsibility should be to question the government. "Is it really necessary to assume that everything the government does has an ulterior agenda?" I say. He argues passionately that questioning the government is the best way for the media to ensure that it is doing its best for the people. "Is it best for the country?" I demand. Suddenly it occurs to me how defensive I become when foreigners make negative comments about China, even though I myself complain all the time about my country. I surprise myself by prioritizing in my question what is best for the country rather than what is best for the people.

I used to laugh about the label of "collectivism" that the Western media often uses when discussing the Chinese people. Who would actually put the collective good over personal interest at every turn? Ironically, however, I have just touched the collectivist mindset hiding in my subconscious, which I have always taken for granted and which has probably shaped my understanding of China's politics. When the former General Secretary, Hu Jintao, made "harmony" the theme of our society, most Chinese people regarded it as a noble goal worth striving for. As opposed to Americans, who sharply distinguish between people and government, we in China subscribe to the goal of the government and its people sticking together to create prosperity. This collectivist mindset accounts for why Mr. Chen takes pride in his job of serving as a bridge and fostering a good relationship between the government and the general public.

David Brooks, a *New York Times* columnist, speaks highly of the Chinese ideal of the "harmonious collective" and implies that it may be "as attractive as the ideal of the American Dream." Drawing on scientific research, he problematizes the Western ideal of individual choice and reckons that the Chinese are right to emphasize the social context. Yet, while collectivism might pave the way for China's rise, a lack of individualism can be a problem. In a course I am taking at the Harvard Graduate School of Education, Monitoring and Evaluation for Improving Educational Systems, one of the biggest challenges we are facing is to find better indicators for education outcomes. Educators have been trying hard to drive the education system ahead, away from industrial education that makes everyone uniform, so that each student today can develop holistically as a unique self. Notwithstanding, the term "individualism" carries a negative connotation of selfishness in China. The notion of expressing one's individuality, though gaining popularity in the 21st century, hasn't fully taken root.

In a recent article, "China's universities must go beyond classroom learning to excel," published in the *South China Morning Post*, fellow Trekker Irene sharply described the differences between Peking (Beijing) University, the best university in China, and Cornell and Harvard:

> During my time there [at Cornell University] — and now

at Harvard—I was able to explore an abundance of non-academic interests… To do all this, I have extended every kind of
deadline, took final exams in foreign hotels, and three faculty committee members scheduled my senior thesis defense
around my needs to ensure I had time for my other commit-
ments.

Everything was flexible to ensure I could direct and maximize my learning—academically and otherwise…this flexi-
bility is afforded to all the other 20,000 students at Cornell.
This is even more so at Harvard.

This, unfortunately, is not the case at PKU. During my
semester on campus, I founded BEAM, a nonprofit that gives
micro-grants to teachers to facilitate innovation in the classroom through project learning…I began to receive invitations
to events and even opportunities to give talks, but had to turn
many down due to scheduling conflicts with academic affairs.
When I was accepted to a highly competitive student conference…I had to jump through hoops to leave campus for
the week…

Reading between the lines, one can easily grasp Irene's idea that
a good education should revolve around the student. Indeed, Western educators believe in the virtues of student-centered education.
Students' academic interests in most American universities are nur-
tured through interactive discussions and collaborative group work,
in which the students themselves have to play a role in leading and
facilitating communication. Students are also encouraged to develop
their own hobbies and other non-academic pursuits. Everything that

happens inside or outside the classroom is designed to make sure that every student gets enough support to succeed.

Such modes of learning and teaching are what I have experienced at Harvard, where students are expected to take the initiative to personalize their own study plan. But they initially seemed alien to me, after my sixteen years' of schooling in China.

The typically large class size in China impedes the interactions between the teacher and students, making introductory lectures the norm, excusing students from participating in the class, and perpetuating their dependence on following instructions. This tradition of conforming to the industrial model of uniformity is detrimental to the country's education system— and even more so to the individuals in that system.

For this reason, I shared Irene's article on Renren (the Chinese equivalent of Facebook) with my friends and classmates: the problems in China's education system should not just be a concern to policy-makers, teachers, and school administrators. Students should know they should not have to do everything by the rules and that they would benefit from actively following their own interests and preferences.

Result vs. Process

"What is the biggest challenge for Shanghai in the next decade, given that it has developed so rapidly over the past thirty years?"

Rachel Loh's question comes in the middle of our meeting with Mr. Chen at Xinmin Media. Mr. Chen jots down some key words in his notebook while I resume the translation. As a former government spokesman who used to hold press conferences on a daily basis, including during the 2010 Shanghai Expo, Mr. Chen is no stranger to this kind of question. He subtly shifts his focus to Shanghai's immense achievements, enumerating all the examples at hand, from the new record of daily passengers on the Shanghai Metro to the opening of the Pilot Free Trade Zone; he doesn't mention the difficulties Shanghai has faced. When he finally talks about the challenges, he says, "We are making efforts towards a quality development in Shanghai, but it is not going to be easy." His term hangs in the air: "quality development."

As the interpreter, I am busy counting zeroes in the figures from Mr. Chen's example. It is not fun switching between two numeral systems, but my past translation experience tells me that Chinese officials like to include lots of numbers. Statistics give them confidence and composure in front of foreigners, so that they can square their shoulders and tell the world that China is heading towards a bright future. It makes our country look good, or as we say, it "earns the face for our country."

In most writing describing Chinese culture, "face" stands out as a crucial part of our emotional landscape. It connotes dignity and perceived social status, and it can be given, lost, taken away, saved, or earned. "To earn face" is a strong driving force in China. High school graduates choose better universities over better majors; college graduates choose big companies over small start-ups. As foreign companies increasingly open offices in Shanghai, a raging fever to work for the "Fortune 500" might explain a lack of original entrepreneurship in the city.

Just as many Chinese people splurge on designer bags for the sake of their labels, the Chinese government lavishes funds on "face projects." Besides those that Mr. Chen has already mentioned, we see plenty of examples during our stay in the city, including the largest artificial lake in the world at Lingang New City (Free Trade Zone), the largest-scale World Expo Site. The Oriental Pearl Tower and Shanghai World Financial Center have not satisfied Shanghai's ambition. Construction on the Shanghai Tower, the second tallest building in the world, is about to be complete, a rapid follow-up to the Shanghai World Financial Center, also called the World's Largest Bottle Opener.

The desire for "face" in Chinese culture echoes the culture's obsession for good results. Extreme competitiveness in a country with a huge population has further strengthened the emphasis on reputation and has diminished the value of process in favor of results.

It is no secret that Chinese students are expert test takers, and yet its top test scores in international standardized testing still stun the rest of the world. We all know that test results should not be the single indicator of educational quality. Nevertheless, in China exam scores and elite status are inextricably linked. Since the establishment of institutional exams for selecting administrative officials during the Song Dynasty, exams have been an inevitable step in social mobility. Education, a term often used to mean simply a good test result, is thus viewed as a means to gain power and wealth.

Today, the College Entrance Examination (gaokao) remains paramount for most students. A good result leads to a good university and a promising career. In retrospect, in no period of my life was I so focused on a single thing as in high school. Three years of marathon studying do not leave much in my memories but dozens of worksheets piled on my desk and equations and endless diagrams on the blackboard. I had to put aside my love for violin and did not have time to think about what I truly wanted in the future.

Struggling to figure out my passions in life during my time at Harvard, I've noticed that unlike most Chinese graduate students who come straight from college, American students typically gain several years of work experience before they apply for a master's degree. With a clear goal in mind, developed from their years on the job, they can get more out of their classes. Thus American students tend to view a graduate degree as a break from work or a tool to change their career track, while Chinese students see it as an open sesame to a desirable career.

In his *New York Times* column, David Brooks once discussed a book on differences between Eastern and Western education called *Cultural Foundations of Learning: East and West*. He summarized its argument in one sentence: "Westerners tend to define learning cognitively while Asians tend to define it morally and socially." I did not understand the sentence until I had the good luck to meet the author of the book, Professor Jin Li. Dr. Li graduated from Harvard seventeen years ago and has devoted her career to studying different cultural learning models and how such models shape children's learning beliefs and achievement. Her research shows that while Westerners tend to see learning as something people do in order to understand and master the external world, Asians are inclined to see learning as an arduous journey they undertake so as to improve themselves. This may be why Harvard students benefit from curricula in which students are allowed and encouraged to enjoy the learning process. But such benefits would not be appreciated in China if they do not yield outcomes considered satisfactory in Chinese culture.

Efficiency vs. Democracy

"All's Well That Ends Well" is my favorite Shakespeare play, not only for its riveting plot but for the wisdom in its title. As long as the result is good, it's worth all the effort of reaching the goal.

Many Chinese people share this outlook on life. It can, however, be a dangerous maxim if it is interpreted as being equivalent to "the end justifies the means." Prioritizing one's end goal is a Marxist belief, and this combined with the fact that China is a Communist country sometimes sends a vibe to outsiders that China is willing to sacrifice everything to achieve its economic growth. That is not true. Though Marxist philosophy is a compulsory course at all levels of education in China, we are never taught to abandon morality and use evil means to achieve good ends.

Similarly, criticizing China for its lack of democracy is common in Western media. In his book, *Billions of Entrepreneurs: How China and India Are Reshaping Their Futures and Yours*, Tarun Khanna, a professor at Harvard Business School, makes an interesting comparison between the two rising powers. He attributes to their different forms of government the fact that China can build a city overnight while India cannot. The book suggests that whereas democratic India has a hard time balancing voices from different sectors and reaching agreements even on small projects like building bridges, the Chinese government does not have to take into account varying opinions before making decisions for the country.

But in fact quite the contrary is the case! The Chinese government is well aware of the severe consequence of upsetting its people. If the government truly turned a deaf ear to its people, by no means could China maintain its economic prospects. As an old Chinese parable tells us, "The water that bears the boat is the same that swallows it." In this case, the water signifies the people and the boat signifies the government. *The Economist* has put forward a similar assertion regarding China: "[T]he regime's obsession with control paradoxically means it pays close attention to public opinion."

During the Trek, many of my fellow Trekkers were curious about my stand on China's politics. I believe that the world needs diversity in its forms of government and that democracy might not be the best form of government for China. For a developing country with a huge population, meritocracy works better than electoral democracy. China needs an efficient system to select leaders with the competence to hit realistic but ambitious targets.

In *Billions of Entrepreneurs*, Professor Khanna affirms the efficiency of the Chinese government. The capabilities of a potential leader are comprehensively evaluated, among them effective decision-making, critical thinking, and the ability to work under pressure or in the face of crises. China's highest decision-making bodies consist of the Communist Party's seven-man Politburo Standing Committee and the 25-member Politburo. All of the members of both groups are selected through a system of meritocracy. The General Secretary must win consensus from the Politburo for major decisions as well as the majority of the National People's Congress. Taking a retrospective look at the history of China, one can see that almost all the constructive policies involving fundamental social change were proposed by the General Secretaries of the Communist Party and their Politburo.

They have accomplished a series of economic miracles by transforming China from a poverty-stricken slum into an industrialized modern nation. In stark contrast, a vast number of developing countries that have adopted electoral democracy are still suffering from poverty and civil strife.

Hard Skills vs. Soft Skills

My father used to quote an old Chinese parable to me as a bedtime story: "If a man carrying half a bucket of water passes you by, you can hear all kinds of water sputtering. If, however, he carries a full bucket of water, it will be much quieter." When it is only half full, the bucket is lighter and is likely to shake back and forth, whereas a full bucket will be steady because it becomes heavier. I grew up believing that truly erudite people avoid showing off their knowledge and that people who talk too much tend to be dilettantes. Among all the Trekkers, I was the quietest. My Chinese gut told me not to throw out careless questions or to offer comments in important meetings unless they were meaningful and well-framed; otherwise, I would be no better than a half-filled bucket of water.

This parable came to mind in our meeting with Mr. Chen, when he said that some Chinese officials do not know how to deal with the media. It is an argument he made to explain the public's possible bias towards government, when Maria Syms (a trekker and a lawyer and government official from Arizona, USA) asked for advice on how to restore people's confidence in their government. Many Trekkers were skeptical about his answer, given that politicians tend to be skilled orators and lobbyists. Even Mr. Chen himself handled the Q&A

section skillfully, suggesting that he knows his way around the media. But his argument is one I can relate to. Whenever I turn on the news in the U.S., I see politicians giving speeches, but when I turn on the TV in China, I usually see leaders smiling and waving. On the rare occasions when they do give speeches, they tend to speak stiltedly, as if reading scripts prepared by their secretaries.

This public awkwardness is a built-in flaw in Chinese leadership. While the elected leaders of the Western world have survived a war of words after running their election campaigns, the Chinese criteria for selecting leaders, although more comprehensive, does not test its leaders' public speaking and communication skills. These are not key qualities that Chinese people look for in their leaders. We might even prefer those who do not speak much, for they seem in consequence more down-to-earth. In a culture where people pay more attention to results than process, actions speak louder than words, for actions are concrete and words are elusive. Most Chinese political leaders study physics, chemistry, or engineering in college, while Western leaders tend to come from majors such as law or other social sciences that lead to greater fluency in public speaking. The disadvantage of having less eloquent leaders, however, is that their stilted speech often makes them appear less creative and spontaneous.

I was therefore surprised on the Trek when we visited Frog Design, a global innovation firm with headquarters in Shanghai, at how positive they are about the creativity of the Chinese people. As one (non-Chinese) senior manager told us: "I've never seen so much creativity anywhere else in the world. But the Chinese just need to learn how to professionalize it." Many parents in China fret that students are graduating without the critical and creative skills necessary to compete globally. There is a growing public concern that our system's highstakes exams and emphasis on rote learning do not cultivate the mental agility and innovative flair needed for preparing 21st century citizens. Frog's confidence in the creativity of this region, however, has changed my perspective. I now believe that Chinese people are lacking not creativity but rather the ability to broadcast their amazing ideas to the people around them.

When I was an undergraduate in China, I saw an article on Renren that poured scorn on a man who got a master's degree from Harvard. The author of the article was upset by the Harvard man's flamboyant speeches on how he had gotten into Harvard, which he gave throughout the country and which had attracted thousands of followers on Weibo (Chinese Twitter). "And guess what?" said the article on Renren. "He is only average in his academic performance in Harvard. What a humiliation to all the Chinese students in his class!" The article got more than ten thousand hits, and most of the comments piled on the criticism. The first time I read the article, I agreed with it fully. However, when I came across this article again last year, I still understood the derogatory comments, but I began to think that they might not be correct. Now that I am at Harvard myself, I've started to think about what defines a truly good education. Here at Harvard, both students and professors see great value in public speaking and the communication of ideas; they care less about the grades that students receive.

In Kuala Lumpur and Seoul, I helped Daniel Wallance, another Trekker, facilitate the Public Narrative workshop, which conveys the message that storytelling and effective communication are critical for great leadership. If you can communicate well and articulate your ideas, you will be able to collaborate with others and inspire groups to face their challenges. Going through all these workshops, I became convinced that Chinese people need to resist some parts of their entrenched cultural mentality and learn how important it is to express oneself clearly and fluently. Being capable in balancing soft skills and hard skills should be a goal for 21st century citizens.

Finding the "Pearl" in the Haze

After two hectic days in Shanghai spinning around conference rooms, we finally got some free time before heading to Hong Kong. I hit the pavement to lead some of my friends on a tour of the Shanghai French Concession in the lovely twilight. As we walked, I started to think about what its "double identity" means to the city. Will Shanghai's march to modernization eventually lead to a clash of two distinct civilizations, or to their fusion?

Just one street away, we ran into the old Shanghai of the 1920s. At that time, Europeans brought a Western touch to the city's original dwellings, and Shikumen (stone gate houses) became a popular choice. A typical Shikumen resembles the traditional Chinese character for "gate," with one or two simple wooden doors in a stone gateway under carved stone patterns. It usually encloses a narrow front yard with high brick walls. In one of these Shikumen houses, the Communist Party was established almost a hundred years ago.

Moving forward, we reached Xintiandi, a vibrant block bustling with nightlife. Fusing the Old and New world, Xintiandi is a tangible embodiment of "east meets west." Brick walls, stone gates, and exquisitely carved wooden balconies can be seen outside the tall Mc-

Kinsey office building. Restored and revamped, with glass-lined walls, this old, tightly packed former residence still keeps its flair, housing modern bars, stylish restaurants, and trendy cafés frequented by Shanghai bourgeoisie.

In Beijing, people think that opening a new Starbucks outside the Forbidden City would ruin the solemnity, but in Shanghai the coffeeshop's green emblem harmonizes with the Shikumen.

Wandering along streets lined with designer boutiques, you know that the city is advancing fast, presumably towards a more Westernized civilization. But the traditional forms of the Shikumen remind passersby that Shanghai is not abandoning its historical identity.

The conjunction of old and new, east and west, reminded me of a message from Mr. Chua Chor Huat, the principal of Science and Technology, one of the Future Schools we visited in Singapore, which have been developed to serve as future models for Singaporean Education. "We want to move closer to the West," he said. "But at the same time, the people in the Western world are also learning from Asia, meaning there are merits in the Asian system. So we do not want to move too fast; we want to move cautiously."

The Western world may stay at the peak of industrial civilization, but the glory of the East can no longer be ignored. The growing number of Chinese students studying in America and Europe is not just a proof of Western charms but is also a demonstration of China's economic growth, which enables more families to afford foreign education for their children. Chinese students like me who are adapting themselves to another worldview while retaining their original Chinese perspective, will bring back fresh insights and add new dynamism while keeping the vitality of the old wisdom. I believe I will be able to synchronize the seemingly incongruous opposites in my life. So will my country.

When Mr. Deng Xiaoping proposed "one country, two systems" during the reunification of Hong Kong, the phrase already hinted that we are determined to resolve these conflicts.

Later that night, we climbed to the top of the Ritz-Carlton on the other side of Huangpu River. Standing on the balcony with a superb panorama of Shanghai in front of us, we are only steps away from the Oriental Pearl Tower. The city's skyline looms out of the darkness, with bright specks of light gleaming from the windows of office buildings. I reach out to hug the pearl, on which neon lights pulsate with great hopes and expectations, which is what "pearl" symbolizes in Chinese. Though the haze does not lift completely, I'm feeling optimistic.

| Chapter 5 |

Shanghai:
The Price of Development?

Margaret McKenzie
MALD, Tufts Fletcher School of Law and Diplomacy

● ● ●

Another Universe

After going to sleep in Dubai in 2013, I found myself waking up in China in 2014. It seemed as if I were entering another universe as, bleary-eyed, I passed through customs at Shanghai Pudong International Airport. I jumped into the taxi to go into the city, and the aroma of old tobacco and previous passengers wafted through the air. The driver was polite and efficient, and as he speeded up, I noticed four odd-looking mobile devices being charged and displayed on his dashboard. A weird mixture of Western music that I had never heard before played in the background. I gazed out the window in a trance at the barren stretch of land lying between the airport and the city. This was my first time in any Asian country, and I tried to take in all of the scenery and every detail. I am a first-year Masters student at the Fletcher School of Law and Diplomacy at Tufts University.

Despite not having spent time in Asia before this trip, I had studied Chinese history and politics, and I thought I was prepared for the Asia Leadership Trek. I had also visited friends in the Middle East: before Fletcher, I was an Information Officer in that region for the U.S. Agency for International Development (USAID). In this role, I communicated the successes of different USAID projects and traveled to such places as Senegal, Dubai, Armenia, Israel, Greece, and the West Bank to learn about USAID-funded projects on the ground. In each country, I had meetings with USAID staff, members of civil society, journalists, and government officials. Having spent so much time traveling abroad, I thought that Asia would be similar and that the trip would be a breeze. I was in for a surprise.

We spent only two full days in Shanghai. What first stood out to me was the juxtaposition between the stark emptiness that lay between the airport and the city and the massive development of exceptionally large buildings and superstructures inside the city itself. Everything moves faster in Shanghai, and the traffic and noise were jarring, contrasting sharply with my family's farm in Canada where I spend each summer—in the small town of Harwood, Ontario, three cars on the street cause a commotion and are considered a traffic jam. As we came closer to the city, I noticed more and more clusters of apartment buildings. As a native of Washington, D.C., I am used to cities with buildings of uniform height. I was stunned by the sight of Shanghai's jagged skyline with towering skyscrapers of all shapes and sizes. In Canada, Toronto is thought of as a large city, with a population size of about 2.6 million, but in Shanghai there are almost ten times that number of people.

The scale of Shanghai was difficult to fathom. I felt like a child lost in a giant amusement park, and even by the end of our time in the city, I still did not have a good sense of where everything was or of any notable landmarks in the city. All I knew was the little map that I carried everywhere of the Pentahotel on Dingxi Road in Changning District. The street signs were in Mandarin, so whenever I needed to take a taxi back to the hotel, I took out the map to communicate where I needed to go. That map was my lifeline to get anywhere, and every time I pulled it out I hoped that my taxi driver would understand it, as I had no other reference. When I lived in the Middle East, specifically in Jordan, I had no trouble getting around by taxi because I speak Arabic. On the Asia Leadership Trek, in contrast, by the time I started getting used to one language we were already in another city; learning anything meaningful in Mandarin in two days is nearly impossible.

But it was important for me to go on this Trek and learn about China and Asia. I wanted to compare my experiences in North America and the Middle East with Asia, which is by far the most dynamic region in the world. Although I severely underestimated the level of culture shock I would experience, I knew that the best way to understand a region's way of life is to connect with its people and experience it holistically, rather than through secondary academic sources. And that is what we did for an amazing two days in Shanghai, meeting individuals from all walks of life.

"Sometimes Efficiency is Not Enough"

On the first morning of our stay in Shanghai, my thoughts drifted back to the barrenness I had seen as I looked outside the cab window on my way into the city. Shanghai reminded me of an Asian version of New York City as it is described in the great American novel *The Great Gatsby*—glitz, glamour, and a culture that constantly changes. Written by F. Scott Fitzgerald, *The Great Gatsby* portrays the 1920s in the United States, an era of economic prosperity called the "Roaring Twenties," marked by social, artistic, and cultural dynamism. One of the novel's major themes is that such prosperity has its costs.

The comparison stayed with me throughout the Trek. In many ways China has become the model for the world: the level of development it has reached in a comparatively short time is nothing short of astounding. Yet, experiencing the context in which China has become the dominant force in the global economy, I was struck by the costs of that development—the price that China has paid and is continuing to pay in order to reach its new position.

Our first meeting in Shanghai was a breakfast meeting, in which we were introduced to journalists and then separated into groups. In my group, I talked to a popular blogger, unique in his role because he covers China's "sandwich generation"— people in their thirties who are torn between three conflicting responsibilities: to their parents, their children, and themselves. Congenial and frank, he talked about the challenges that his generation is facing as they support multiple generations. He also gave his take on the situation in China: "The government and people are efficient in the work that they do, but because things are developing so quickly, sometimes efficiency is not enough."

Not enough for what? Perhaps he was alluding to the lack of pensions for the elderly or the high costs of educating children; but his comment resonated with me in another way. Efficiency has done an admirable job of taking hundreds of millions of people out of poverty, but it often has consequences, a few of which are rural-urban inequality and environmental pollution. Due to these and other problems, the number of protests in China doubled between 2006 and 2010, when there were 180,000 reported mass incidents, according to the Chinese Academy of Governance.

Speaking about the challenges the government will face, the blogger said, "China will change at the next elections because the labor will be more expensive." The reality of rising wages foreshadows a different growth model, one with important implications. China's landmark urbanization plan from 2014 to 2020 will shift away from investment and towards a more intensive growth model based on private consumption. A *Xinhua News* report said that, "Domestic demand is the fundamental impetus for China's development, and the greatest potential for expanding domestic demand lies in urbanization."

Clearly the subsequent challenges of urbanization, along with the government's alleged need for heightened censorship, will compound the potential for unrest. When one of the Trekkers asked the blogger about censorship, he acknowledged the issue but pointed out that the Internet is now changing the situation. Surveying all of us at the table, he said, "We want more transparency—that is the desire of this generation." An open and transparent society is the result of a healthy relationship between the media and the government. But in the next meeting on our agenda, I would learn about the buffering role that media plays between China's leaders and its people.

Sage Kings and the Art of Censorship

After our meeting with the journalists, we traveled to the headquarters of Shanghai's largest media company, *Xinmin Evening News*, to meet with the editor-in-chief. When we arrived at *Xinmin's* building in Shanghai, we were greeted in the lobby of the building and escorted up to the top floor, where we took pictures of the striking, albeit hazy views of the Shanghai skyline.

Xinmin Evening News is the oldest newspaper in China. It was founded in 1929 in Shanghai and is Number 43 on the rank of global daily newspapers (according to the World Association of Newspapers). The news agency boasts a circulation of over one million. We visited their headquarters in Shanghai on Weihai Road, but they also have bureaus in Beijing, Shenzhen, and Los Angeles.

Entering a briefing room, we saw two walls lit up in red and white letters that wrote out "Welcome 'Asia Trip' Delegation" with the translation in Mandarin underneath, matching the bright red font of the company logo. We passed room after room of busy journalists scuttling among the cubicles, scanning social media websites, and designing bright red and white documents on large, flat-screen computers. When one of the Trekkers asked a staff escort about censorship in China, she was greeted with an awkward silence and a change of subject. Such a conversation had to be held with the appropriate person.

We were then escorted to another boardroom with a large wooden table, comfortable white chairs, and large paintings of mountains on the walls. Chen Qiwei, the chief editor of *Xinmin* (and the appropriate person), was waiting for us. Before his tenure as the Chief

Editor of *Xinmin*, he had spent five years working as a government spokesperson in seventeen districts of Shanghai and forty-five bureaus of China.

The first question directed towards him had to do with censorship. In his calm and direct response, Mr. Chen said that the media has the right to criticize the government. He noted that some Western people may have the impression that the media in China is under strict control. However, as the editor-in-chief, he has the final authority to decide what can be reported to readers. With remarkable nuance, he explained his argument that every freedom has a limitation and that there is no complete freedom anywhere. He pointed out that media outlets need to abide by certain criteria, in which they should hold themselves responsible both for individuals and for the larger society. He also said that there had been an increase in government accountability as a result of Xinmin Media's coverage on problems with housing policies and other current issues. Governors of provinces are now accountable to the media, which they must deal with in their everyday decisions.

Despite the nuances in his language, it became clear to me that Mr. Chen's previous position as a government spokesperson colored his views on the government. Defending the government's leadership direction and choices, he noted that no other country has accomplished more than China in the last thirty years. Although he admitted that the Chinese people now face many problems — namely social and environmental issues and a loss of culture — he maintained that the government was doing a good job in controlling economic growth.

In my eyes, censorship was a steep price to pay for development. It seemed absurd to me that a former government spokesperson could hold a position in which he is responsible for being a voice for the people—the same people who might want to criticize the establishment. Nevertheless, if I took what Mr. Chen said in good faith—that he "wishes to serve both the government and society"—then the message he sent indicated a completely different mindset on the issue of censorship. According to this mindset, the Chinese are living within a "sage king" society, in which those in charge rule by virtue and wisdom. If that is the case, Mr. Chen's defense of their censorship—one that is to be relaxed over time—makes sense.

The more essential question, though, is whether or not individual ambitions are being constrained by this lack of freedom under the government. I began to wonder if Chinese citizens were hopeful about their future—and the next day provided me with ample opportunities to answer that question.

"There Is Nothing You Can't Do."

"With a good education and hard work, there is nothing you can't do." Mrs. Michelle Obama's words in a 2009 TED talk echoed in my head as we rode the bus to the "High School Affiliated to Fudan University." Mrs. Obama's statement embodies the classic ethos of the American Dream. In 2013, Chinese President Xi Jinping described his own country's new doctrine, the "Chinese Dream": "national rejuvenation, improvement of people's live-lihoods, prosperity, construction of a better society, and military strengthening." With an obvious nationalist bent, he said that young people should "dare to dream, work assiduously to fulfill the dreams, and contribute to the revitalization of the nation."

When we arrived at the gate of the school, we were each paired with a student, and we traveled in groups of ten people. We saw their museum of student and teacher art, played basketball with students, and received a full tour of all the buildings. I wondered what life in the students' dorms were like, if they had freedom and were cognizant of world events. According to one student, the Arab Spring was covered in Shanghai and the students had held a discussion forum on the issue.

Their knowledge of the events in the Middle East surprised me. In early 2011, when I was living in Jordan, a Chinese journalist had come through Amman and stayed with my roommates and me for a few days, when the Arab Spring was at its worst. I remembered him going into detail about how little the Arab Spring was being covered in China. He said he had tried to publish contentious material about the situation, but the Chinese government would not allow much of the material to be published because it might have given local Chinese people the idea to protest as well.

Of course there is very little chance that the students we met that day would protest. They represent the cream of the crop in China and have little incentive to gather and demonstrate. But considering that students led the previous movements in China, I was still astonished by how aware these students were of local and global events, and how eager they were to ask questions.

During group sessions, many of the students we spoke to said they wanted to become entrepreneurs. Others mentioned professions such as engineering and journalism. As opposed to students in the United States, at Tufts Fletcher and even at Harvard, these students were confident that they would have job opportunities once they graduated. I thought back to the students I had worked with in Jordan. They lived with their families and will live the same lives as their parents unless they move out of the country. In contrast, the students at Fudan seemed independent and ambitious, with futures likely to be more prosperous than and removed from their parents' lives. The upward trajectory of the middle class in Asia became real to me.

Although I was speaking only with the best and brightest in China, I assumed that their confidence at least partially reflects the confidence felt by the hundreds of millions lifted into the middle class of China. These students have better things to do than complain about a lack of freedom. According to a 2013 Pew Survey of Global Attitudes, 85 percent of Chinese were "very satisfied" with their country's direction, compared with only 31 percent of Americans. On the whole, the Chinese government is able to tackle their problems directly and efficiently, and people in China are quick to point out that the government does not "shut down" like the United States's government over disagreements. It is not difficult to see why the rest of the world is looking to China as a model to follow.

Nevertheless, I could not let go of a nagging thought. Everywhere I went, I was reminded of it by the smoggy air that surrounded me. Despite the benefits of fast-paced development, the unpleasant byproduct of environmental degradation in China was obvious. How sustainable was the country's fast-paced development for future generations?

The Good Earth Project

After our school visit, we hurried to the other side of town to Xintiandi, where we met Mr. Chris Shallis of the Good Earth Project. The name of the project is a reference to the 1931 novel by Pearl Buck *The Good Earth*, a book that evoked American sympathy for China in the 1930s.

Mr. Shallis' organization combats environmental issues on Chongming Island in Shanghai. Black rice grows all around the island, and the farmers typically have to spray pesticides for the rice to grow. The Good Earth Project, however, raises crayfish to eat the eggs of the rice pests around Chongming Island, thus removing the need for pesticides.

I learned from Mr. Shallis some disturbing facts about the worsening state of the environment in China. These facts showed why his work was so essential to the future of China. For instance, Shanghai's water census listed 53 percent of the water as Grade V—in other words, "dead water." That means that eight million acres of water, an area the size of Indiana, is too polluted to farm. Nor does the worsening environment in Shanghai stop at polluted water—it includes poor air and land quality as well.

Because of China's exponential growth, there has been a shift from a producer-driven economy to a middle-class consumer culture. Yet the government is failing to mitigate the devastating environmental effects of this growth. High-energy consumption, high-polluting heavy industry, and massive concentrations of air pollution cause a number of human problems—48 percent of businesses in China said they have difficulty retaining talent because of the country's air pollution. And according to the World Health Organization, more than 500,000 pollution-related deaths have occurred in China since 2008.

The environmental cost of development in China is damaging

the quality of life for its people. It is the government's job to regulate a country's environmental standards. For instance, since coal is the main polluter of air quality in China, contributing approximately 80 percent of the country's carbon dioxide emissions, why are cleaner fuel alternatives not promoted and carbon dioxide emissions not taxed by the government? Can fast-paced, unrestricted overconsumption be justified in a socialist market economy? This question stuck in my mind as we entered the office of the affluent architect Ben Wood.

Shanghai's Power Broker

Described by *The New York Times* as a "Shanghai power broker," Mr. Ben Wood is an American architect who came to Shanghai in 2003 to redevelop Shanghai's iconic Xintiandi District. He is also one of the most interesting, imaginative, and multi-faceted people I have ever met.

As we made our way into Mr. Wood's dimly-lit office, I noticed an assortment of unique objects—drones, 3D printers, a hodgepodge of art, and a table with a number of model airplanes on it. He gave us a brief presentation about his work in redesigning Xintiandi District, and then he showed us a number of slides of his many houses and the places where he gets his inspiration. He showed us, for example, the Rome flood plaza, which they would flood with water in the afternoon to keep it cool. For all of his accomplishments, he seemed quite humble and pragmatic.

Although Mr. Wood is not a Luddite, he believes in keeping technology to a minimum. He showed us homes with many windows, homes surrounded by trees, and various other buildings that save energy and keep cool without the need for electricity. He pointed out that three- or four-story buildings are the most practical to build, whereas skyscrapers, though they are all the rage now, have no redeeming qualities except "looking like a piece of a man's anatomy." Mr. Ben Wood is the face of the achievement potential of fast-growing China, but although he tries to help preservation by making his new buildings similar in appearance to the city's traditional structures, Shanghai's landscape is inevitably being altered to keep up with the rapid influx of people.

Underlying his work of creating remarkable spaces, Mr. Wood's philosophy balances history with innovation. By avoiding politics and any controversy that could harm his career, he has been able to make a fortune from the unprecedented development of Shanghai. As we sat cramped in his crowded office, he boomed, "In China you can do anything you want." He discussed how the country's limited regulatory oversight allows him to be unimpeded in his projects. The same limited oversight that is causing major environmental problems in China, such as an 80 percent increase in cancer deaths from smog. Mr. Wood, however, has found an individual freedom in China that he did not have in the United States, and he complained of the regulations in the United States, saying, "America is broken. It is overregulated."

Ironically, the man who embodied what most impressed and worried me about China is an American. It was surprising to me that he was so critical of the United States and yet ignored the glaring social and environmental problems in China. Perhaps this is because Mr. Wood seems to have grasped his dream in China. It is clear that he is doing what he loves, and he has an assortment of stories, luxurious houses, and possessions to prove it.

Our meeting with Mr. Wood raised more questions for me, such as the paradox of human freedom and fulfillment under government control and regulation. Mr. Wood has found that he can do more in China than he could in the United States, yet the lack of regulations has proven to be both environmentally and socially harmful.

The Valley of Ashes

Cynical thoughts whirled through my head as we drove, exhausted, to Pudong Airport. I began thinking again about *The Great Gatsby*, which not only describes the dynamism of the Roaring Twenties but also serves as a warning, reminding the reader of the dark side of decadence and excess. Shanghai seems unstoppable in its growth, and on the surface, one can see the benefits of that growth: not only has the city reduced the level of poverty, it has improved access to education and healthcare and has seemingly increased overall wellbeing. Inevitably, however, growth slows, and when it does you are left with the consequences.

In a "universe of ineffable gaudiness," to use Fitzgerald's phrase, it can be difficult to see beyond the dazzling display of glitz. Yet some people in China are becoming increasingly wary of their country's growth and have also thought to compare it to *The Great Gatsby*. A young Chinese blogger recently noted that Gatsby's world was a world of "mobsters running wild, farmers leaving their land, rushing toward the big cities on the East Coast, farming life declining… Money inscribing itself on morality." The blogger realized that "these are all the very things China is facing today." In America's history, the

Roaring Twenties was followed by the Great Depression—and after researching Shanghai and China extensively, meeting with numerous media figures, students, businessmen, and experts in the city, I came to believe that censorship and environmental degradation would be just a few of the human costs for development in China.

During the ride to the airport, I was reminded of the Valley of Ashes so memorably described in Fitzgerald's novel. It was pouring rain, and the scenery around us was reminiscent of the desolate landscape between Manhattan and the East Egg—created by the dumping of industrial ashes and representing the moral and social decay that results from the pursuit of wealth. There was a dirty and gray feeling to our surroundings outside Shanghai. The only thing missing were the frowning, god-like eyes of Doctor T.J. Eckleburg looking down on the highway from a billboard, cautioning the people below.

My two days in Shanghai represented just a cross section of what is a definitively modern city that embodies a world rendered all the more complex by the competing influences of rampant pollution and industrial growth; urbanization and emergent opportunities; and flagrant excess and upward mobility. While my observations of a pocket of Asia did not polarize me to one perspective of how sustainable economic development is achieved, I was reminded that every governmental choice is accompanied with caveats that may undermine the basic pursuits of welfare. Shanghai has attained monumental achievements that belie the constraints we assume in the United States. As such, I agree with my peers in academia who admonish China's heady growth but I also recognize the pragmatism of those whose endeavors are confined to the opportunities of the microcosm in which they live.

| Chapter 6 |

Discovering Creativity in Asia

Raymond Ko

Ph.D. Harvard University

● ● ●

When scientists get together, they love to talk about theories and solutions—and not just in the arena of academic research. As a PhD candidate in Biology at Harvard, I enjoy talking with my colleagues about many different issues, from business and policy to education and human rights. Here I must say, apologetically, that many of us, especially at Harvard, do think we are smarter than the average person. When we come across stories of politicians making what seem to us hilarious mistakes, we will ridicule them and say something dismissive: "Why don't they just execute plans A, B, and C? Then the problem would be solved in a few months."

As outside observers, we tend to oversimplify problems due to a lack of information. Quite a lot of us, including Harvard scholars, think we can develop solutions after reading only a cursory amount of background information in the news. To us, it seems that many nonscientific problems in the real world could be simplified, divided, and conquered accordingly, if only they were handled by the "right people."

Today, it's common for policy makers, business leaders, and teachers to have achieved a level of education that qualifies them for their jobs. They have often trained at the best schools in the world—and even if they don't come from a "reputable" school, many of these leaders are as smart as we are and frequently much smarter.

In reality, most situations are more complicated than we can imagine, and often such complexity becomes an obstacle to simplifying the situation. In some cases, the complexity itself is an important element of the issue. If we remove the complexity and focus on only one or two pieces of the puzzle, our understanding of the problem will be biased and we will not be open to the possibility of multiple solutions.

So how do we remove our "bias-colored glasses" to see these diverse, real world issues accurately? Finding the answer to this question was one of my central purposes when I embarked on the Asia Leadership Trek, which provided extremely valuable opportunities to meet with people I wouldn't have had the chance to meet had I traveled alone. They included students from local schools, staff from major corporations, and executives of international firms, each of whom gave different perspectives and insights on the same issues. Their insights served as scattered pieces of a puzzle that we tried to gather and assemble into a larger vision. Although the entire picture will never be complete, we still move closer to a full understanding.

Before coming to Harvard, I spent four years in Beijing, where I completed my bachelor of science degree at Tsinghua University. It was at Tsinghua that I experienced the true meaning of craziness:

students spending nealy all their waking hours studying, keeping extracurricular activities to a minimum.

Needless to say, I am a product of that exam-oriented education system. The common belief is that this system of education does not create innovators. Even students like me, successful in climbing up the examination ladder, believe that there are better ways to develop our talents and creativity. I am enthusiastic about scientific research, so I hope other science-loving students in Asian countries can fulfill their potentials, discover the beauty of knowledge, and use it in impactful ways, just as their Western counterparts are doing.

Coming after "the age of information," the phrase "age of innovation" has become another buzzword and spawned a lot of discussion. Innovation is the way to a bright future for a student, a company, or even a country. In a highly competitive world, one needs to provide new, differentiable values to gain a competitive edge and distinguish oneself from others. Creativity provides the major source of those differentiable values.

Although I am not an expert in the area of creativity, I saw this Trek as a valuable opportunity to learn about creativity in an Asian context. I wanted to learn what academic and business figures had to say about the topic. Though I knew I was not going to develop policy solutions, I did know that I would come away with a better understanding of the real, everyday issues facing actors on the ground in Asia. In the process, I also learned a little more about myself.

Ideas from Different Places

The student was at the end of his first semester at Tsinghua University. As he walked into the meeting room of the biology department, he sat down with seventy-seven other nervous students. Tension was in the air. For twenty minutes, he listened to the masters students, who served as mentors to the freshmen, congratulate them on a great semester and offer advice for the next one. But all of the freshmen were waiting for one thing.

The mentors handed out long strips of paper with the following information: Name. Student ID. Average score of all courses. The most important item was the next one. The student looked at his paper and blinked a few times. "Rank in the department: 73 out of 78."

He felt small, as if his dignity had been laid bare on that piece of paper. Deeply ashamed, he spent the next few weeks desperately figuring out how to succeed. He learned that there were many tricks to achieving high scores. Visiting during office hours right before the exam, equipped with loaded questions to trap the teaching fellow into giving clues on the exam question? Check. Asking older students to recall exam questions and diligently recording their answers to save for next year, when he would take the same class? Check.

I know this student well—he was a close friend of mine at Tsinghua. Throughout his career at the university, instead of learning subjects deeply and applying his knowledge creatively, he learned instead how to cheat creatively. This system of education, focusing on so-called "results" rather than on actual learning, blocks off nearly all avenues of creativity. As a result, horrifying as it may sound, the student's methods of cheating were one of the most creative aspects of his life. He encountered a problem and came up with an out-of-the-box solution to solve it. He learned how to be practical and resourceful—but not in the way his teachers intended.

As this example demonstrates, such a system of education ultimately holds schools back. The anecdote illustrates the primary problem that many schools in Asia are facing. This student's primary goal was not to learn the content of his courses and apply it creatively. His primary goal was simply to maximize his exam grades, regardless of what means he used. Yet if schools in Asia adopted instead the goal of creating innovators in different fields, then the creativity this student showed in cheating would have been directed towards his work itself, guiding him onto a more productive path.

My experience on the Trek showed me multiple ways that schools in Asia are using to solve the problem of encouraging and directing creativity.

Shanghai: Fudan High School

Led into an exhibition hall by six students at Fudan High School (its full name is "High School Affiliated to Fudan University"), we gazed at hundreds of amazingly professional art compositions made by the students. They then gave us a full tour of the school, bringing us to a wood-floored basketball court, a room with ping-pong tables, a three-story library with both Chinese and English works, and, finally, to a computer lab with fifty of the latest Apple computers. I was extremely envious; the facilities in my prestigious high school in Hong Kong could not compare with these. Even some of the computers in the labs at Harvard did not match the computing power of the Apple computers I saw at Fudan.

The diverse, world-class facilities demonstrated the school's serious commitment to developing a fun, dynamic, and interdisciplinary environment for its students. One of the Fudan girls told me in Chinese, "The pressure of examinations is definitely not small, but still we enjoy the life and education here." Even though they looked a bit shy, the students had their own, independent opinions on various social issues, from air pollution to education reform, all backed up with logic and evidence. Chatting with them was like talking with mature college students. More importantly, they looked happy, energetic, and excited.

Fudan High School combines the rigor of exams with an interdisciplinary approach. The principal of Fudan High School proudly told us about his strong team of teachers, many of whom have PhDs. He also mentioned that these enthusiastic teachers guide students in their many student organizations, from debate teams to Model UN. More surprisingly, at the start of each semester, students choose from over one hundred elective courses offered alongside the core courses. These electives cover a wide range of topics, from arts and languages to innovative projects led by professionals in various fields. By allowing its students the freedom to pursue their interests, Fudan makes sure that they are not only prepared for exams but also exposed to diverse areas in the liberal arts. This ensures that they can be confident, well-rounded, and sensitive to different perspectives, all qualities nece-ssary for creativity.

Singapore: School of Science and Technology

Similar to Fudan, the Singapore School of Science and Technology (SST) is a school blessed with abundant resources arising from significant government investment. Both Singapore and China have provided large sums of money to test their pilot education programs.

SST's biomedical laboratory fascinated me. I was amazed to see experimental apparatus usually found only in universities and research institutes, including fume hoods for tissue culture and PCR (polymerase chain reaction) machines, a very expensive tool for DNA replication that is necessary for DNA manipulation. This PCR machine is something that most high schools around the world simply cannot afford. It was mind-boggling to me that high school students would have the chance to operate one. I learned from SST's principal, moreover, that it isn't only in biology that the students receive this kind of support; they enjoy similar resources in other fields too, including physics, chemistry, media, and technology.

SST's strategy is built upon the theory of the critical period, which holds that if you learn a language or a motor skill early in life, you will be more skilled at that task in the future than those who learn it later in life. At SST, students develop their interests and start exploring their potentials in specialized areas from an early age. SST's investment of $20,000 Singaporean dollars (USD $16,000) per student allows students to operate specialized, frontier technology. SST hopes that this will put their students on the cutting edge of knowledge, with a future advantage in the field of innovation.

Hong Kong: Lee Shau Kee School of Creativity

When I heard that we were going to visit the Lee Shau Kee School of Creativity in Hong Kong, I did not know what to expect. Entering the gates, a small team of staff and students greeted us. Two of the female students had dyed hair and dressed like cartoon characters from a Japanese anime. I'm a big fan of Japanese animation, but this was the first time I had ever met real "cosplayers."

It was clear that students are not required to wear uniforms at this school. Having gone to a conservative school in the same city, I was shocked to hear the students call their teachers by their first names, even the principal. After visiting their performing arts theater, student galleries, and many studios for video, dance, art, design, and technology, we came to a room where the students showcased some of their films, one of which depicted the lifestyle of the elderly within the context of a changing Hong Kong. The teaching staff's enthusiasm was palpable. Later, when a Trekker asked a student what his parents thought about his choice to pursue a career in music, the student answered, "I think I'll be okay, because, well, my parents are hippies." Everyone erupted in laughter, including the teachers.

The Lee Shau Kee School of Creativity emphasizes a culture of collaboration. Their nontraditional policies and norms create an environment that allows free expression and the flow of ideas, breaking down barriers between students and teachers. This culture allows for a level of communication that helps to create value out of ideas.

What I Learned From Our School Visits

Ultimately we cannot really tell which of the above strategies is most effective. Or, rather, we should not be restricted by the mindset that one strategy is better than another. A mixture of the three strategies would probably work best: combining exams with liberal arts, giving kids a head start with frontier technology, and providing a great culture in which students can feel free to express themselves.

No matter which approach one prefers, one should always take into account the local environment and conditions and be ready to experiment with different strategies.

Inspiration from the "Kissmas Tree"

As I strolled through the shopping alley of the affluent Xintiandi district, I noticed a small crowd of people around a forty-foot Christmas tree. I wondered what the commotion was about. A couple, holding hands shyly, walked up the steps towards the tree. As the crowd looked on, I could feel anticipation in the air. The couple stood facing each other, each instructed to hold a branch of the tree. They looked at each other, their bodies slowly moved closer together, and they shared a long kiss.

When the connection of the kiss completed the electrical circuit, the lights on the "Kissmas Tree" began sparkling beautifully. Ten years ago, the idea of Christmas and even the concept of kissing publicly were not common in China. The willingness to embrace foreign cultures and ideas has definitely contributed to the creativity of Chinese and many other Asian cultures. Just as the lights on that Christmas tree came from the couple's kiss, inspiration can come from unexpected places. On the Trek I learned that creativity does not come only from the education one receives at school.

After admiring the "Kissmas Tree" we visited Studio Shanghai nearby, where Mr. Ben Wood, the architect responsible for Xintiandi's redevelopment, welcomed us warmly. His workshop was packed with a huge variety of handmade models, from robots to drones to miniature houses. His inclusive approach of incorporating history, culture, and function into redeveloping Xintiandi has become so successful in China that the word "xintiandi" is said to be a verb among developers, as in, "Can you 'xintiandi' this project for me?"

After showing us pictures of his many homes, hobbies, and spectacular projects all over China, he said, "China is the land of opportunities. It is even okay for you to talk about air pollution, education, food poisoning... As long as you don't touch the sticky stuff like politics, then you can do whatever you want in China."

One vivid example he talked about was the design of drones for nonmilitary purposes. "In the States," he said, "due to the inflexibility of the laws and regulations, asking for the permission to build drones would have taken years." He then showed us a picture of himself standing next to a completed drone model. "But in China you just go ahead and get the job done within months." He explained that a pragmatic approach is typical of local and foreign designers and businessmen in China. The lack of regulations in certain fields unleashes the freedom to create prototypes, thus stimulating innovation.

With the final question of the day, I asked him, "How did your group come up with so many creative designs? How do you inspire yourself?"

"Observation," he laughed. "I just spend time walking down the street, and I become inspired. I look at everything around me, and I observe. I do this at least once a week, and I strongly encourage my colleagues to do the same. You need to be sensitive and always be ready to learn from everything. You need to be inspired by the environment around you and by the talents of other people."

I have been in academia for my whole life, and as a PhD student I spend most of my time in the lab or in the classroom. In the past, whenever I've had conversations about creativity with my friends, especially those at the Harvard Graduate School of Education, we talked only about developing creativity in schools. I'd always considered the concept of creativity in an academic context. But in observing Mr. Ben Wood and his many projects, I realized that creativity should be seen not only as a process that can be learned in the classroom but as an approach to life.

Earlier that day we visited Frog Design Company, a global product strategy and design firm with its Asian headquarters in Shanghai. We talked with General Manager Mr. Steve Boswell, who conducted a workshop for us based on Frog Design thinking. I asked him how difficult it was to recruit staff in China, given that the country's students study under a rote learning system. He answered by saying that recruiting qualified locals was easier than he had expected. What he said next stunned me: "I've never seen so much creativity anywhere else in the world."

In the education workshops I had attended with my fellow Trekkers at the Harvard Graduate School of Education, we had had long discussions about exam-oriented education killing creativity in Asian countries, including China. So what was going on here?

After some reflection, I realized that despite the inhibitions that a classroom education can inculcate, all aspects of life have the potential to encourage creativity. A person's environment and the policies—or lack thereof—that shape that environment are crucial factors in the development of that person's creativity.

On the Studio Shanghai website, they lay out their beliefs:

> [T]he building of habitable structures is not an exercise in theoretical design or a prescient inspiration of an individual designer or architect. Instead, we work with culture, climate, physical and spiritual elements, and flora and fauna of the region to make places that help people know where they are,

and by extension know who they are. In other words, we are dedicated to creating places in which people feel they belong.

Environment as much as education can unleash creativity. Thus, in addition to more innovative schools, we also need to create spaces that inspire creativity. For example, when we walked into the offices of Studio Shanghai and Frog, I sensed an ambience that both intrigued and energized me, an atmosphere created by pictures of the staff hanging on the walls, recycled materials used as coffee tables, sofas placed next to individual workstations, and, most important of all, workers who did not wear formal suits but instead sported outfits that expressed their individuality.

Most of us who live in cities spend ten to twenty years in school, but we spend even more years of our life in workspaces after we graduate. Obviously, therefore, the workplace is one of the major locations, if not the most important one, where creative ideas are generated and then translated to business or social values.

The development and maintenance of creativity is a life-long process. New ideas don't arise only from nine-to-five. They happen at all times of the day, in the most unexpected places. Scholars of education frequently talk about different methods of enhancing the creativity of the next generation through education in schools and universities, assuming that creativity can be cultivated only in schools. But we should not forget that innovative working environments and living spaces, appropriate regulation policies, and the shaping of a receptive culture can contribute even more to the creativity of both individuals and whole nations.

The Real Purpose of Creativity

"I felt like I was not valued by my peers, teachers, family, or even myself. In school, I did badly in everything. In life, I did not achieve anything. I was useless. Every day was the same, and I could not break from that pattern…"

The above quote is from a local student I met while on the Trek, who described what her life was like studying under a competitive, exam-based education system. As this system only values those who can memorize well and thrive in a zero-sum world, it wastes all other talents and does not allow individuals to improve their world in non-traditional ways. The sole units of success, according to this system, are exam scores for students and money for adults. Unfortunately, the diverse talents of many students cannot be translated into grades. These students become the losers under this system.

The argument for creativity and innovation in society is often framed in economic terms. One prevailing question among commentators is "Why are successful, innovative giants like Apple and Google born in the United States but not in China?" Often they then point to the exam-oriented education system as the root cause of the lack of creativity and innovation in China. But maybe that is not the right way to look at it. Does it make sense to think of creativity only in terms of a return on investment?

While we were at the Lee Shau Kee School of Creativity, fifteen students formed a panel to share their experiences in the school. After tearfully relating a horrendous experience she had undergone in a previous school, one of the girls said, "Now my life has transformed. I do not necessarily have a 'big dream,' but I know what I want to do.

My ideas and efforts are valued. I can freely explore and fulfill my potential. Simply put, I am alive."

Most of the students shared the same sentiments. Their stories made me rethink the deeper purpose of creativity. I had been viewing creativity in economic terms, and that is usually how it is judged by investors and other figures in business. But after talking with these students and seeing how fulfilled they felt in the accepting atmosphere of the Lee Shau Kee School, I realized that the underlying purpose of creativity is something far greater than financial success: creativity allows people to feel alive, not merely as drones in a larger system but as independent individuals with their own voices, values, and ambitions; and this is why creativity is an invaluable and powerful force.

Ultimately, this truth was the most important thing I learned on the Trek. Visiting actual places and talking with actual people not only allowed me to understand the complex issues surrounding creativity in Asia, it also made those issues more personal for me.

I have been a scientist for most of my adult life, but I am interested in pursuing business consulting in the future. In both fields, the path to solutions is always undetermined. And in both fields, the same thing excites me: discovery. When faced with a problem, I become enraptured by following the path towards new answers. It is my natural curiosity that drives me.

From my Trek experience, I discovered that creativity is limitless. I saw this in the creativity that innovative schools in Asia are using to come up with unique solutions to achieve their mission of thorough and forward-looking education.

Creativity is also all-encompassing. I learned on the Trek that it encompasses all aspects of life, from the workplace to the home, from education in schools to lifelong learning.

Most significantly, I also learned why we are creative. We create because by doing so we allow our spirit to achieve its natural purpose, to strive towards that which is limitless and all-encompassing. By doing so, we feel alive.

| Chapter 7 |

Singapore:
A Nation in Transition

Rachel Loh
MPP, Harvard Kennedy School of Government

● ●●

"As you look at the threats and possibilities, you consider the following options: Singapore could remain an undeveloped agrarian society with small traders, pig farmers, rice growers, and fishing villages. Nobody would have to change...A second option would be, as the communists in Singapore had been advocating, to become an anticapitalist, protectionist state and align Singapore with India and China—as many other countries have done in this postcolonial period....

"Another option is to get the people to take on the tough work of making themselves better, more educated, more skilled, and more industrious. If you could do that, your people might get good jobs, earn high salaries, and enjoy a better standard of living, possibly advancing to the level of first world countries, although that seems a real stretch..."

— Professor Dean Williams

In one of my favorite classes at the Harvard Kennedy School (HKS), Professor Dean Williams led a discussion on Singapore's development challenge when it first gained independence in 1965. The above excerpt is from Professor Williams' book *Real Leadership*. It profiles Mr. Lee Kuan Yew, Singapore's first Prime Minister, and the leadership challenges he faced. Underlying Professor Williams' course is the philosophy of "adaptive leadership," a framework developed by his fellow Harvard professors Ronald Heifetz and Martin Linsky. The philosophy defines leadership as the "activity of mobilizing people to face reality and tackle the tough problems by doing the 'adaptive work' necessary to achieve progress."

Fifty years ago, the adaptive work in Singapore consisted of many development challenges: unemployment, poverty, low educational standards, ethnic factions, and communist unrest, to name only a few. None of them had easy solutions. And solving one of them, let alone all of them, seemed like a "real stretch."

Much has changed in Singapore since that time. Indeed, Singapore has survived as a sovereign state through sheer grit and its ability and willingness to deal with rapid change. I was excited that it was one of the five cities on our Trek because our visit allowed me to see Singapore from a different perspective after my first semester of studying at the Kennedy School. Although we were in the country for only two days, I wanted to take the opportunity to examine and reflect on its development. Beyond its achievements, I also wanted to learn what its leaders had to say about the way forward for Singapore in a future in which its qualities of survival will continue to be severely tested.

Singapore became my home more than a decade ago. Just a four-hour drive from my hometown of Kuala Lumpur, Singapore was often a quick weekend getaway for my family. My earliest memories are of the brightly lit Christmas trees and wonderful window displays of Santa and his elves that dazzled us on Orchard Road. After those early holiday trips from Malaysia, its poorer neighbor, I was fascinated by the country's juggernaut economic progress, its carefully planned urban infrastructure, and its efficient government bureaucracy. Twenty years later, the country continues to amaze me with its relentless transformation and its desire to remain relevant on the world stage, despite being only a "little red dot" on the map.

Singapore is an island city that first gained prominence as a British trading port, so it comes as no surprise that maritime metaphors often find resonance here. Leaders have often likened the nation to a "sampan," the Malay moniker for a shallow, flat-bottomed boat often used by fishermen in the region, to emphasize how Singapore, much smaller than her neighbors, is all too vulnerable to being tossed about by the winds of global politics and competition.

Barely larger than the five boroughs of New York City put together, Singapore first unmoored itself from British colonial rule by hitching its fate to that of the newly formed Federation of Malaya (later renamed Malaysia) as the Federation's fourteenth state in 1963. Irreconcilable differences in politics, however, including ideological disagreements in affirmative-action policies for the ethnic Malay majority, led Singapore to be cast adrift by the larger Malaya in 1965.

Singapore's then Prime Minister, Mr. Lee, broke the news of Singapore's independence on television in a tearful announcement. His party, the People's Action Party (PAP), quickly consolidated power with the aim of national development. With the nation on its beam-ends, it was critical to get everyone rowing in the same direction. An implicit social compact emerged between the government and the populace, in which the government agreed to deliver material prosperity in exchange for the people's uncritical support.

I have heard stories from taxi drivers about this challenging time. They recount the uncertainty of being a newly independent nation, but they also speak of the resilience and hard work of their generation. Many were immigrants from China and India, for whom feeding their families and having a roof over their heads were their main priorities. Singapore's leaders recognized these sentiments, and that is what allowed them to mobilize the people and face the country's challenges as a unified group. For the people, there was no reason to rock the boat as long as their essential needs were met.

The System Simply Works

We arrived at Singapore Changi Airport late in the evening. The airport is modern but not ostentatious, rationally designed, and immaculately clean. The immigration officers speak English; they are polite but also curtly efficient. It is virtually impossible that one would encounter a shakedown for bribes at immigration here (or anywhere else in the country, for that matter). Walking out of customs, we were pleasantly surprised to see our luggage ready for us at the baggage carousel. Within thirty minutes of stepping off the airplane, we were already seated on a bus on our way to the hotel. After the relative chaos of American airports and security lines, it was a telling reminder of the comforts of Singapore life.

As Changi runs, so runs Singapore. Even at the airport, one receives a revealing glimpse into the country and a reflection of its governing philosophies. The impression we got coming into the country was that we were safe, that we would be taken care of, and that the system simply works.

In the early 1960s, Singapore asked to join Malaysia partly because its leaders wanted access to a larger domestic market. Their thinking was that import substitution industrialization (ISI) was the most reliable way for a country to develop economically. Singapore's population then was only 1.7 million, so its leaders thought that a customs union with the much larger and resource-rich Malaysian market would be critical to the viability of Singapore's economy. When Singapore was unceremoniously kicked out from the Malay union, however, it had to rethink its industrialization strategy.

In the years after independence, Mr. Lee and his cabinet knew that Singapore's survival would be dependent on its economic development. The many challenges facing the country meant that philosophical niceties in policy were an unaffordable luxury. The country had to implement whatever worked. Thus was born a culture of pragmatism, one of the things that Singapore subsequently became famous for.

Recognizing that it did not have the necessary capabilities to pull its economy up by its bootstraps, Singapore became one of the few countries in the world to actively court foreign talent, training, and investments. Singapore's openness was evident in its immigration policies. Mr. S. Rajaratnam, Singapore's first Foreign Minister, envisioned Singapore as a "global city" and welcomed anyone with the capability and willingness to contribute to Singapore. Singapore also sought advice from whoever was willing to assist its growth. Dutch economist Dr. Albert Winsemius, Mr. Lee's economic advisor, led the United Nations Survey Mission to examine the country's potential for industrialization. Soon Singapore partnered with countries like Japan and Germany to set up training institutes to cater to the needs of their own companies.

The country offered multinational corporations a stable investment environment to set up production. For those companies willing to commit to invest in Singapore for the long term, the government offered attractive tax breaks and other forms of support. Courting these corporations could not have come at a better time, as the 1960s saw a wave of outsourcing from advanced economies.

The presence of multinational companies raised the quality of Singapore's industries. The government continued to identify new growth sectors moving up the value chain, each decade focusing on the pursuit of new growth sectors. Today Singapore hosts over seven thousand multinational companies. Electronics, petrochemicals, biomedical products, and pharmaceuticals are all vital arteries of the Singapore economy. At one point in the 1980s, Singapore was producing over 80 percent of the world's hard-disk drives. Today, Singapore makes more than 90 percent of all offshore oil exploration rigs, despite being such a small country.

The attitude of pragmatism revealed in Singapore's early economic policies also pervaded other aspects of government. Very early on English became the language of government and administration in Singapore. The politicians astutely recognized that English would become the global language of business. This was in contrast with the official Malaysian policy, in which English was shunned as a colonial vestige and Malay was adopted as the official language.

The PAP was unapologetically ruthless about removing impediments to national development. Corruption was rooted out at all levels of government, including within the party. Criminal elements were severely dealt with. Much land was forcibly acquired for development. And a myriad of national campaigns were conducted to promote behavior congruent with the aspiration of becoming a developed country: there were campaigns against littering, against public urination, for family planning, for courtesy, and for speaking proper English, among others. After I moved there, I soon forgot to notice that the convenience stores did not sell chewing gum.

Throughout these often difficult changes, the PAP received unwavering support from the people at the ballot box. The collective benefits were obvious to all. Living standards improved tremendously, and many Singaporeans rapidly ascended to the middle class. The strength of this social compact between the government and the public was a key factor in Singapore's success. The system simply worked.

Best Man for the Job

"There's no better way to run a country than the best man for the most difficult job."

- Lee Kuan Yew

Early on, the Singaporean government knew that their country had little room for mistakes and that the best minds were needed to help run the country. To identify and cultivate such talent, Singapore decided to adopt meritocracy as a core philosophy.

In Singapore, civil service jobs are generally well remunerated and seen as desirable; cabinet positions are among the most highly paid jobs in the world. Regardless of other qualifications, jobs in government after independence were given to those best suited for them. As a corollary, the government also streamed people through the education system to identify the most gifted students. These star pupils were given the resources to succeed.

In this sense, Singapore probably comes the closest out of all countries in approaching the ideal of Plato's Republic, where the governed are ruled by an elite class of "philosopher kings" who decide what is in the best interest of the people.

The World Bank has consistently ranked the Singapore government highly in terms of its effectiveness. I was humbled to work with such amazing talent when I was at the Singapore Economic Development Board (SEDB) and the Singapore Tourism Board (STB). My fellow Trekkers also experienced this effectiveness through our many meetings in Singapore. In our conversations with Mr. Poon Hong Yuen, Deputy Secretary for the Ministry of Law and former Chief Executive of the National Parks Board, and Mr. Lionel Yeo, Chief Executive of the Singapore Tourism Board—both of whom had served many years in the civil service—we were impressed by how much foresight and innovation the government used in planning policies. Despite the governmental bureaucracy, one of the key factors to their success was the cohesiveness of the public service, which "seamlessly functioned as one public service in a unified and coordinated team supporting each other"—a whole-of-government approach, as described by Mr. Yeo.

The dilemma latent in Plato's Republic is the question of who will keep the philosopher kings accountable. Yet thus far the success of the Singaporean model seems to make this a moot point. While being Asia's least corrupt government by several measures, GDP per capita in Singapore has grown more than a hundred fold, from just slightly over USD $500 in 1960 to over USD $50,000 today in nominal terms. The country has also accumulated outsized foreign reserves through consistent budget surpluses, and it has the most well-equipped and well-trained military in the region. It is Asia's least bureaucratic place to do business, according to the IMD World Competitiveness Rankings in 2011. The Mercer Survey of 2011 ranked it as the country with the best quality of life in Asia. According to the Deloitte 2013 Global Manufacturing Competitiveness Index, it is the world's number one for math and science education. The World Bank's Doing Business 2012 Report deems it the world's easiest place to do business and the second most competitive city in the world. The list goes on.

It must have given many people in Singapore, especially those who had lived through Singapore's early days of independence, a sense of validation in 2011, when Bloomberg magazine reported that Singapore's GDP had surpassed that of Malaysia, a country almost five hundred times larger and blessed with many natural resources. The "sampan" of Singapore had become an agile speedboat.

Keeping Busy:
Industriousness and Individual Responsibility

On our second day in Singapore, we visited the Lee Kuan Yew School of Public Policy to attend a lecture and speak with a few academics. Arriving at the garden-like campus of the school, which is under the National University of Singapore (NUS), my thoughts harkened back to an earlier period; I walked through the corridors of the school's colonial-era buildings and thought back to my own early days in Singapore, when I attended NUS. My economics professor at that time shared a story with the class to illustrate the industriousness and personal responsibility of the Singaporean people. He poignantly described how his seventy-year-old father was continuing to work each day at McDonald's. Despite the best efforts of his son, who urged him to "just retire," his father wanted to keep busy.

The meritocratic society of Singapore values self-reliance and individual responsibility, and it frowns on idleness. It is perhaps unsurprising that there is a big emphasis on individual responsibility when it comes to social policies in Singapore. My taxi-ride conversations often revolved around these unique policies — from the pension scheme to healthcare and education policies, all vital cogs in building a self-reliant population. Sometimes the drivers were critical, but underlying nearly everyone's comments is the basic understanding that hard work brings good results.

These values are represented in the government's antipathy towards certain public welfare spending initiatives. Instead of a national pension, each working person in Singapore contributes a portion of his or her salary towards a personal account in the Central Provident Fund. In addition to buying an annuity after retirement, funds in this account can be used to pay for housing, education, and medical expenses. As a result of this forced saving, home ownership rates in Singapore are well over 80 percent (comprising mostly government hou-sing), and government expenditure on healthcare as a percentage of total healthcare costs is one of the lowest in the developed world, even while the quality of care is one of the highest. Singapore's universal healthcare system is based on a hybrid model, with government subsidies, compulsory savings, and price controls within the public health system. To ensure against the over-utilization of healthcare services, no public medical service is provided for free, regardless of the level of subsidy, even within the public healthcare system.

One of the few areas in which the government has deviated from its philosophy of public welfare spending is education. After defense, education commands the highest share of government spending, as education is seen as the most effective way to promote social mobility. Many of the Trekkers were surprised to learn how much the government spends on education in Singapore. When we visited the Singapore School of Science and Technology, we learned that the government spends about 20 percent of the annual national budget on education funding. Singaporean children have access to affordable and high-quality public schools up to at least the secondary level. Tertiary education, some form of which is available to those who want it, is also subsidized.

Besides education, public services are for the most part operated strictly according to market principles, although the government does provide targeted and means-tested subsidies for housing and healthcare. The public is expected to pay fair market prices for services consumed—from utilities to public transport. Direct social transfers are available on a limited basis, but they are heavily means tested.

The Changing Tides

"The social contract was essentially this: Singaporeans accepted the PAP's hold on power, accepted the restrictions of political and civil freedoms in exchange for good housing, good jobs, a decent education system, and a high quality of public goods. And that social contract is beginning to fray...partly because society's demands are a lot more diverse, a lot more heterogeneous, a lot more pluralistic and complex."

The above quote came from our conversation with Mr. Yeoh Lam Keong, Adjunct Senior Research Fellow at the Institute of Policy Studies and former chief economist of the Government of Singapore Investment Corporation, and Mr. Donald Low, Associate Dean for Research and Executive Education at the Lee Kuan Yew School of Public Policy. Despite the success of the social contract between the Singapore government and its people, it is still, as Mr. Low says, "not sufficient to ensure equitable and inclusive growth in the face of the changes unleashed by globalization, rapid technological change, and Singapore's own policies."

What is ironic about Singapore today is that many of the problems it faces are a result of its own success. Singapore continued to grow strongly in the 1990s and 2000s. However, side effects of this rapid growth became manifest. The country's population expanded rapidly from four million in 2010 to 5.3 million in 2012. Singapore's favorable environment and low taxes attracted the globally mobile. One high-profile example is Facebook's co-founder and billionaire Eduardo Saverin, who renounced his U.S. citizenship in 2011 and now lives in Singapore. Having the highest density of millionaires as well as high net-worth individuals, Singapore also became the country with the highest number of luxury cars per capita.

But increases in rapid growth and population strained the infrastructure of the country. Public transport became crowded, and housing and other costs of living rose rapidly, in many cases faster than wages. I myself rented an apartment with an annual lease, and every time the lease was up for renewal, I dreaded the possibility of having to move due to higher rent. Thankfully, the rent increases were manageable, and I moved only twice in seven years. In the country's non-stabilized rental market, however, some of my friends were unfortunate and experienced rent increases of up to 40 percent from one year to another.

In the early 2000s, with the rise of the Internet and social media, a newer generation of citizens took to online spaces to air their grievances. Many felt that their leaders, who had risen through Singapore's unique system of meritocracy, had become "elitist" and unable to empathize with the struggles of the average Singaporean. The high pay for politicians became a lightning rod. Others pointed to the increasing signs of class segregation in the country: the children of well-off families attending different schools; the availability of private medical care for those with the means to pay; the price of private housing versus government housing and cars that because of taxes were becoming increasingly out of reach for the average Singaporean; and the increasingly visible signs of poverty. A new generation of voters, more demanding of their leaders, were unafraid to voice their dissatisfactions. Some asked if the rapid rate of economic growth came at too great a cost to their quality of life. It was a narrative I had not heard before, though I had lived for years in Singapore.

Then came the 2011 general election, which Singaporean author and social commentator Ms. Catherine Lim described as a "watershed election." Eighty-two out of eighty-seven seats in Parliament were contested, the highest number since independence. For many Singaporeans, it was the first time they could cast their vote at the ballot box: many constituencies in the prior elections had been left uncontested due to the lack of candidates from opposition parties. The PAP suffered its worst ever showing at the polls, receiving 60.1 percent of the popular vote and winning eighty-one out of the eighty-seven seats. In any other country, this would be considered a land-slide—not so in Singapore. To the PAP, used to popular vote shares of 70 to 90 percent, this was a stinging rebuke and an omen that all was not well in its relationship with the electorate.

In a 1994 essay published in Singapore's only English daily, *The Straits Times*, Ms. Lim labeled the phenomenon a "great affective divide," observing that the electorate lacked any real warmth or affection for the party despite being grateful to it for Singapore's continued economic success. It seemed as if this divide had widened further since it was first identified.

In the aftermath of the 2011 general election, the PAP convened a committee to review the salaries of politicians, which resulted in wage reductions of up to 30 percent for some appointments. The government also greatly increased spending on public housing, healthcare, and public transport, tacitly admitting that it had under-provisioned for the rapid increase in population. The price of government housing was explicitly unpegged from market prices in order to make it more affordable.

During our Trek meeting with Mr. Devadas Krishnadas, Managing Director of Future-Moves, a Singaporean strategic risk consultancy, he explained, "It was necessary for the government to recalibrate the balance between state and market, between social protection and individual responsibility." The result of the re-calibration has been a gradual adaptation of policies to help older, low-, and middle-income Singaporeans cope with the rising costs of living.

Recognizing that segregation in education had also become a contentious issue, the Ministry of Education set out on a program of reform to achieve the goal of "every school a good school" and to set limits on fundraising by independent schools. At the same time, it continued to pilot specialized schools to increase the diversity and variety in the education system. We visited one of these schools and spoke with its Principal, Mr. Chua Chor Huat. We could see how passionately he encouraged his students to become entrepreneurial and innovative thinkers. Such schools pilot new ways both for tea-chers to teach and for students to learn.

This same drive and passion was evident during our meeting with Professor Tan Oon Seng, Dean of Teacher Education at the National Institute of Education, who is committed to grooming highly skilled teachers who are effective in instilling critical, creative, and analytical thinking in students from all schools. He opined that a critical factor in a child's development is the engagement of parents. To that end, schools and teachers need to encourage the active participation of parents in their child's learning.

The government also made many pronouncements that none of the less fortunate in society would be left behind, launching a series of reforms to social welfare policies and making a commitment that no healthcare would be denied based on the inability to pay. A focus on "growth" by the Ministry of Trade and Industry was modified to a focus on "inclusive and quality growth."

When we met Mr. Laurence Lien, the CEO of the National Volunteer & Philanthropy Centre and a nominated Member of Parliament, he explained, "Civil society needs to step up and do much more to help meet the increasingly complex needs of the Singaporean community." He argued that the non-profit sector could play a much larger supporting role in the Singaporean government's efforts towards social progress and development.

It's still too early to tell if all of these efforts to win back the electorate will prove successful. Some early signs are encouraging: many have voiced their appreciation of having a bigger say in government policies. However, both the ruling party and the administration are still trying to find their sea legs in this new environment. While the tone of the government has become softer and more compassionate, some new policies still seem to be marred by old habits of top-down thinking, such as new licensing requirements for online news portals and the launch of a Population White Paper projecting a 6.9 million population by 2030, both of which received strong opposition from the public.

Brought up on tales of political infallibility, the current generation of voters might well have unrealistically high expectations of their leaders. At the same time, the electorate is no longer cut from the quiescent mold of voters that politicians have gotten used to. If this period of change is to be managed well, both the governed and the elected government will have to negotiate a way of working well toge-ther for the good of the nation. This negotiation will involve a fine and delicate balance. Singapore cannot indiscriminately abandon the many policies in industry development, education, healthcare, and social welfare that have made it one of the best countries in the world to live in.

The Course Forward

While at Harvard, I sometimes wondered if Singapore's well-oiled, efficiently run government would be able to steer successfully into the unchartered territory of the future. And as I reflected on this question during the Trek, I realized one thing: of all the conversations that we had on the Trek with political, educational, business, and media leaders, those conversations held in Singapore were by far the most real, honest, and candid. What was also interesting was that the HKS alumni we met in Singapore cited the philosophy I recognized from my course at Harvard, "adaptive leadership," as what Singapore needed to move forward.

Singaporeans know changes are needed. As Mr. Low at the Lee Kuan Yew School of Public Policy said, "Leadership is all about change. If you're not in the business of change, don't bother being a leader." In the past, the Singaporean public has viewed its leaders as always having the answers. But the most recent generation of leaders has recognized that they may not have all the answers. They acknowledged Singapore's problems and were willing to tackle them head on, with the intention of working collectively to find a shared solution.

I am optimistic for Singapore's future. The country will remain relevant because it wants to remain relevant. The Trek allowed me to see this desire both within and outside government: everyone we met was hoping for a better and more inclusive Singapore. Singapore has shown incredible resilience and ingenuity in tackling its challenges.

The years after its fiftieth anniversary in 2015 will be no different. Compared to other countries in the region, Singapore's future looks remarkably promising, however critical the Singaporeans themselves might sometimes sound: Singapore has a highly educated population, a strong network of global economic links, a world-class albeit slightly crowded infrastructure, a fiscal position the envy of many other countries, and a sterling reputation for business and governance.

Though it must navigate between domestic tensions and global challenges, Singapore will stay the course. The people of a country that was once written off as a sinking ship have proven to be great captains, and they will no doubt continue to steer their ship well.

| Chapter 8 |

The Questions We Ask:
Stories of Efficacy and Resilience

Karol Mark Yee
Ed.M., Harvard Graduate School of Education

●●●

I have always worked in the background. Before coming to Harvard, I spent my days as a "back-staffer," which means sitting behind my boss during meetings and public hearings.

I worked for Senator Edgardo J. Angara, the longest-serving Senator of the Philippines since our country reclaimed democracy from the hands of the authoritarian leader Mr. Ferdinand Marcos. An astute, self-made man from a virtually unknown province in the Philippines, my boss made a name for himself by becoming a lawyer, then Head of the Integrated Bar, then President of the University of the Philippines; eventually he rose to become President of the Philippine Senate. Called "Mr. Education," he authored a set of laws from the 1980s to when he retired last year that essentially put in place the general structure of the current Philippine education system, from early childhood to basic, tertiary, and technical-vocational education.

He worked us hard. Despite the decades between us, my boss

had the energy to start his day at 4 a.m., and he filled each one with speeches, back-to-back meetings, public hearings, and working meals, all without missing a beat. Because I was a backstaffer, my schedule was more or less the same to his: I reported sometimes as early as 6 a.m. and turned in, like him, just before midnight.

One of the reasons I joined the Asia Trek was that I missed that life: the rush of running between meetings, having casual conversations with policy-makers, and being a fly on the wall—spending time with national leaders and hearing about what bothered them.

My other reason for coming on the Trek was to find out why the Philippines is lagging behind other Asian countries in terms of its development and economic success.

Every time there is a public hearing in the Philippine Senate, the Senators look at indicators of how the country is faring—in such areas as gross enrollment rates, maternal mortality, and farm-tomarket road ratios—compared to our neighbors, among them Shanghai, Hong Kong, Malaysia, Singapore, and Korea. In recent years the most important yet implicit question for lawmakers and ministers in these analyses has been "Where have we gone wrong?"

Many still reminisce about the golden years of the Philippines in the 1950s and 1960s, when we were the "most envied country in Southeast Asia," as our National Artist for Literature, F. Sionil Jose, has said, when South Korea was "battered and poor after the Korean War of 1953," and when Kuala Lumpur was "a small village surrounded by jungle and rubber." None of these statements hold true today.

These days, when Filipinos look at themselves in the mirror, they tend to see a "damaged culture" instead. In 1987, following the

EDSA Revolution that removed Ferdinand Marcos from power, an American columnist, Mr. James Fallows, came to the Philippines and claimed that it would be next to impossible for the country to turn itself around—at least in this lifetime. To make his point, he quoted an observation from Benigno Aquino, whose assassination in 1983 led to the 1986 revolt that ended with Mr. Marcos in exile and Mr. Aquino's wife, Mrs. Corazon Aquino, establishing a new government, which today is headed by their son, Benigno III.

Mr. Aquino said: "Here is a land in which a few are spectacularly rich while the masses remain abjectly poor... Here is a land consecrated to democracy but run by an entrenched plutocracy. Here, too, are a people whose ambitions run high, but whose fulfillment is low and mainly restricted to the self-perpetuating elite."

The problem was, according to Mr. Fallows, that the Filipino culture was a "damaged culture" in which "the national ambition is to change your nationality."

I have often wondered if this is still true. In some ways, joining the Trek was a chance for me to confirm or disprove this perspective on the Philippines: has the country lagged behind through mistakes of its own making? How did the obstacles of its now developed neighbors stack up against those faced by the Philippines? Did their worries measure up to the Philippines'own worries? After all, the Philippines has been colonized by three countries and driven into debt by a dictator; it faces an ongoing rebellion in the south and a looming conflict with a Goliath named "China." When I set out on the Asia Trek, I hoped that in asking the question, "Where have we gone wrong?" and hearing about the stories of our far more successful neighbors, I could gain a better understanding of this decades-long assumption.

Being "In Relation To" China

Coming from the Philippines, I myopically thought that China mattered only to Filipinos, given our worsening territorial disputes and our minimal military strength. But because of China's increasing political and economic dominance, I realized during the trek that many governments have likewise been forced to position themselves in relation to China in order to keep themselves relevant, among them Hong Kong and Korea, despite the economic strength of both those economies.

On the Trek, during our meeting with the unexpectedly down-to-earth President of the Legislative Council of Hong Kong, Mr. Jasper Tsang, we began to understand Hong Kong's position as a Special Administrative Region (SAR) of China, and the challenge they faced in keeping their niche as the leading financial center in the region, especially with the expansion of Shanghai.

Despite its own colonial history, being taken from China by the United Kingdom and then given back to China in 1997, Hong Kong seems to know itself, possessing a sense of identity that allows it to position itself with confidence in an increasingly competitive global economy.

Tug-of-War between Past and Future

For all their success, South Korea struck me on the Trek as a country still struggling to find a balance between dealing with their past and confronting their future. It was very apparent that the question of whether they will face reunification or war with North Korea is a common topic of conversation for South Koreans—and the possible advantages of reunification vie with concerns over the cost of such reunification to the Korean economy. This tension between North and South is visible not only on a figurative level but literally, thanks to the fences and military establishments just a few hours from Seoul that are meant to hinder the invasion of North Korea in case a war erupts.

In spite of these worries, the South Koreans continue to push forward, imagining a future for Korea with what they have called a "creative economy." They hope to leverage the creativity of Korean youth and the booming technology scene to sustain unparalleled economic growth. Yet it seemed to me that while many of the initiatives laid out by the Korean government (among them streamlining processes for patents and establishing innovation labs), were admirable, they also seemed lacking. For example, the Korean education system is known to rank high in the PISA (Program for International Student Assessment), an exam taken by students from all over the world that tests proficiency in math, science and reading), but it is common knowledge that the Korean education system remains rote and traditional.

It could be that they are still in the early stages of this transition from a knowledge-based to a creative economy, thus these "birth pains" of figuring out how to best go about it. But nevertheless, because their leaders are able to ask the right question, that is: "How can our economic success be made sustainable for the future?" I feel confident that in the same way they transformed their country from being a donee to a donor country in a matter of decades, they will again prove the naysayers in us wrong.

After our group photo-op at the National Assembly, Rep. Hwang

Woo-yeo, head of the ruling Saenuri Party, smiled at me and asked if I was Korean. I said: "No, actually I'm from the Philippines." He then smiled even more broadly: "Philippines," he said, "you helped us a lot during the Korean War. Thank you."

I was moved because the war had taken place over half a century ago, in the 1950s, and yet his sincerity was as palpable as if it had happened just last year. I was also surprised not because of his gratitude but of my not knowing this even happened: Filipinos learn many things in history class—about our struggles for freedom under the colonial regime and then under our own dictator—but very rarely do we celebrate moments that can give us pride. It startled me to remember that as recently as the 1950s, the Philippines were not the ones struggling against a superpower but were instead sending military help to our neighbors. Seeing our flag there at the De-Militarized Zone between North and South Korea as one of the "first responders," I admit to feeling a mixed sense of pride, but also of hope: for the day when we can move back from weakness to strength.

A Struggle Towards a Truer Democracy

"The problem is that even if we make our national universities great, I cannot get in," said a Chinese student in an open forum that we held with Malaysia's Secretary General of Education, Dr. Zaini Ujang. The comment was met with the applause of hundreds of students in the gymnasium. Coming from Southeast Asia myself I found this tension between the students and the government representatives at this forum surprising: direct confrontation of leaders in Asian countries happens rarely, after all. We later learned that the tension that unfolded before us was brought about by a decades-long affirmative action instituted by the government: one in which opportunities in both education and work have been reserved for Malays, effectively easing out the Chinese and Indian populations in a highly racially diverse society.

While this affirmative action has, as we learned, gone on for years in Malaysia, the encounter in the gym and several other conversations after gave me the impression that resistance to the policy is gaining ground with the advent of a more outspoken youth and the freedom granted by the internet (in comparison with government-controlled broadcast and print media). Despite the tight grip of the ruling coalition party, which has governed the country since it gained independence in 1957, opposition is growing, and there appears to be a strengthening, albeit still disjointed, move to work towards a more equal and democratic society in Malaysia.

A recurring theme in our conversations in Malaysia was that of "squandered potential"—many people we spoke with recounted past glories of a country that has been blessed with many advantages but has not lived up to its potential. As a result, while we found budding optimism among the Malaysians, it was still shaky and seemed in need of nurturing. Challenging a ruling party that has been in power for decades takes persistence, one which could become the litmus test for Malaysia's new generation of opposition leaders. It will not be long before we find out if they are able to rise to this call.

The Malaysian narrative of "squandered potential" is similar to the Philippines' narrative of a "damaged culture." Of all the countries we visited on the Trek, Malaysia with its worries seemed the closest to my native land. I discussed this similarity with two Malaysian friends who were also on the Trek: we wondered if the similarity existed because of a shared tendency to dwell on the past and its failures or because of a shared ability to recognize inherent greatness in two countries that have not yet reached their full potential. Perhaps the answer lies in both.

Renegotiating a (Very Successful) Social Contract

"The social contract in question is this: in 1965, after their independence from Malaysia, Singaporeans agreed to accept the great power held by the People's Action Party (PAP) and the restrictions on political and civil freedoms that the PAP imposed, in exchange for good housing, good jobs, a decent education system, and a strengthening economy. The contract proved both highly successful and satisfactory to both sides for over forty years. Recently, however, the agreement has begun to fray, partly because Singaporean society's demands have become a lot more diverse and pluralistic, and partly because the government's ability to ensure rising social mobility, affordable public housing, and a strengthening economy is beginning to come under strain." These words came from a commentator in Singapore.

Before I arrived in Singapore, I found it difficult to understand how its citizens could still have worries, given that it has one of the highest GDPs in the world and arguably the best education system in the region. I have visited this island-state many times in the past decade and have always admired the great progress they have achieved, not to mention, respect for Mr. Lee Kuan Yew, whose visionary leadership is well acknowledged by many in the region. To my surprise, however, when I arrived in Singapore I found that the discussions we had there were more philosophical than in many other countries we visited prior: despite the success of their social contract, many Singaporeans now view the system as outdated and no longer appropriate for dealing with the needs of today.

While there remains great admiration for Mr. Lee, the original architect of this social contract, many people are explicitly speaking of a renegotiation. During our conversations, a recurring theme was a need for less technical solutions and a call for an expansion of political and social policies: among them, healthcare and early childhood education. And these gaps, according to the academics we talked to, exist despite Singapore's capacity to become a welfare state in the tradition of the Nordic countries, given its 5 to 6 percent GDP surplus. Another criticism of the current system is the lack of freedom for the press, in an era of global information flows and communication—a realm in which Singaporeans are conspicuously silent.

Thus, while reaping the rewards of its first generation of leaders led by Mr. Lee, policymakers in Singapore today are grappling with the evolution of their country's culture and the increased demand for social policy. I could sense their worry about transition in government leadership, particularly over sustaining the country's advantages in the coming years while still allowing for reform.

For many Singaporeans this sustainability rests in the hands of a new generation of leaders who can skillfully and knowledgeably steer the country, as they do today, but also listen to and empower their own people—breaking this so-called "strong dependency mindset"—referring to a tendency to accept passively all the government's decisions. Essentially, in spite of the success of their own government, a growing number of Singaporeans want to have a bigger stake in their own country's affairs and to be a part of shaping their own futures.

Unlike President John F. Kennedy who roused a nation by telling them to "Ask not what your country can do for you, but what you can do for your country," in Singapore, the clamor seems to come from the people telling their government, "We want to do something, let us."

The Questions We Ask Ourselves

At the end of the Trek, I asked myself once again how and where the Philippines had gone wrong in the quest to strengthen its political, economic, and social systems. Once again I sought the reasons behind the Philippines' "damaged culture."

In one of the Trek's meetings in Singapore, when I asked a prominent economist how Filipinos could work with the existing institutions in the Philippines to bring about change, he responded, "You have a different problem. The Philippines' issues are much more complicated than the ones we have. You'll need bloodshed to change how things are right now."

This was hardly a vote of confidence. Yet, reflecting on this conversation on our flight home, I realized that what had struck me in Singapore and in all the countries we visited was people's unwavering faith in themselves: in each country, the people we spoke to believed that they could pull through—and so they do.

When Korea was trying to rebuild itself after the Korean Civil War, with a sluggish economy and a divided country, they were able to revive their economy and come out stronger than they had ever been. Today they are asking themselves how they can make their success sustainable and are putting the weight of government behind creating a "creative economy," while everyone else is still working towards a "knowledge-based economy."

In Malaysia, I learned an essential lesson from one of the country's leaders. During our talk with Dr. Zeti Akhtar Aziz, the current Governor of Bank Negara Malaysia, the Malaysian central bank, she told us that in the aftermath of the damning Asian Financial Crisis of 1997 she and the other financial leaders of Malaysia decided to introduce a unique exchange control strategy. Initially the strategy came under fire from bankers and experts all over the world. A year of great international pressure tested Dr. Aziz's resolve. She described moments when "what seemed to be a light at the end of the tunnel turned out to be an oncoming train." Nevertheless, she stayed focused on her goal, refusing to "be distracted by the great noise around us." Such focus requires not only great courage but a steadfast knowledge and faith in one's self. In the end, her resolve paid off: the strategy restored stability to Malaysia's financial system.

Lastly, though they were leading a new country with no natural resources, a population of migrants, and a contentious past, Mr. Lee and his fellow founding fathers gave life to the unknown island-state of Singapore, which has since become one of the most important economies in the world. Today, undaunted by the double challenge of past achievements and future uncertainty, Mr. Lionel Yeo, Chief Executive of the Singapore Tourism Board, responding to the many challenges that continue to come their way in a rapidly evolving and competitive tourism industry, answered: "It's never been done before, but we're Singapore. We'll do it."

In the Harvard Graduate School of Education, one of the core concepts I learned in many of my classes is that of "self-efficacy," the belief in one's abilities to succeed. It is so important that researchers sometimes use it interchangeably with the word "power.". In the school setting, evidence shows that teachers can tailor the curriculum, provide all the books, and even revise a teaching style to help a particular child, but if that child does not believe in his or her own ability to succeed, all the teacher's efforts will be in vain.

So does the Philippines suffer from a fatally damaged culture? After going on the Asia Trek, I believe the answer is no. The country's history speaks of the capacity of its people to resist centuries of colonial power, to challenge a sitting government and effectively take down leaders who have not served the interests of its people, as well as to actively engage in public discourse and push for social policies for improved healthcare, women's rights, land reform, and reproductive health, even amidst the constant battering of hurricanes and natural disasters.

Are Filipinos a people who is tired of trying, making them less confident in the face of adversity? Perhaps: particularly when it comes to the broader reforms that have since become binding constraints to the country's growth.

F. Sionil Jose, one of my favorite Filipino authors and a man who has written much on the Philippines' national identity, culture and poverty, once claimed, "Power will always elude the very poor until they believe what that poor Spaniard cried out during Spain's Civil War: 'In my hunger, I command.'"

The stories of Korea, Malaysia and Singapore speak to this truth: that in the face of adversity, despite threats of hunger, war, and constraints in natural and human resource, the ability of a people or a nation to believe their capacity to command, is what ultimately gives them the ability to.

Therefore looking towards the future, instead of asking, "Where have we gone wrong?" a better starting point might be to ask "How can we succeed?" And in this commanding phrase, finally author a worthy resolution and dénouement to the much-extended Filipino story of efficacy and resilience.

| Chapter 9 |

Meeting Malaysia's Entrepreneurs

Nikki Skovran
MBA, Harvard Business School

● ●●

In complexity, difficulty, and reward, entrepreneurship is like raising a child. It is all-consuming, with moments of joy and despair in rapid succession, as every meeting and phone call can be a moment of success or failure. Like parents, entrepreneurs nurture their ideas, slowly developing them in their mind; they seek advice from every possible source to learn what works and what doesn't; they save money in anticipation of upcoming costs. In Malaysia, I met the entrepreneurs Mr. Victor Lam, Mr. Ng Kay Yip, and Mr. Warren Leow Jia En.

Each transfixed me with tales of failure, resilience, and success. Although their stories varied greatly in both length and experiences, entrepreneurship was the common thread of their journeys.

As unexpected issues arise and the entrepreneur tries to control the project at hand, he or she realizes that not everything can be learned in books or from mentors and begins making many decisions on faith, hoping they are the right ones. Over time, as an idea grows and becomes successful, the entrepreneur needs to enlist additional resources to help with day-to-day product management. The idea grows and blossoms, changes and matures, and eventually the entrepreneur can see the rewards of the energy and commitment put into the business. My Malaysian entrepreneurs are each at a different stage of this process. Mr. Lam is still in the idea stage, garnering resources in anticipation of his product launch. Mr. Leow has just launched his company and is trying to get his product off to a good start. Mr. Ng has gone through the process in its entirety, with a couple of successful products under his belt.

Learning about the experiences of these three innovators and hearing how they are navigating the world of entrepreneurship helped me to understand Malaysia's culture and character, the challenges of its entrepreneurial landscape, and the hope of its people.

At the Kids' Table

Hundreds of students dressed in business-casual wear were moving about in the open-air setting of Sunway University. While the event staff shuttled up and down the stairs, I sat at the registration table being bombarded with questions. Our Trek was hosting the conference, "21st Century Malaysia: Public Leadership, Education and Entrepreneurship," and I was one of the organizers. It was here that my impression of Mr. Lam, one of the local helpers, was fully formed.

From the moment I arrived, Mr. Lam was at my side, helping me. He executed one task after another, anticipating what we would need and completing it, often before I even asked. At one point, when I didn't have a specific task for him, he brought me coffee, knowing that I hadn't had a moment to pour myself a cup. Our common purpose was to deliver an impactful conference.

"Mr. Lam gets things done," I thought. "How perfect that we are at a conference about entrepreneurship, full of people just like Mr. Lam — getting things done." Entrepreneurship and innovation at their core are about doing something, trying to create something new, often in the midst of a chaotic environment.

In a much quieter setting at the Teach for Malaysia office, I had a chance to talk with Mr. Lam one-on-one. He is tall, with dark short hair; his glasses and neatly pressed button-down shirts give him an academic, intelligent look. He has a kind, assertive voice — confident but not aggressive. I asked him about entrepreneurship as a career in Malaysia and the challenges facing him and other Malaysians.

"The biggest personal challenge is that people find it really hard to break away from the comfort of the safety that a job in the corporate sector or a family-inherited business provides. I think there are a lot of people who want to be entrepreneurs, but they are pressured by many sides, including themselves, to not make the leap."

Mr. Lam himself has already taken a step towards entrepreneurship. Instead of joining a big firm or a multinational corporation, he joined the social enterprise Teach for Malaysia. While it provides financial stability in a structured setting, his job also allows him to build his skills and network. Importantly, it is a place where he can let his ideas marinate. While working here, Mr. Lam spends his free time talking to entrepreneurs, investigating startups, and dreaming of a future in which he runs his own business. He knows that his stint at Teach for Malaysia is only temporary and that someday he may face the difficult choice between stability and passion.

I asked him about the barriers that hinder students and professionals from choosing entrepreneurship as a career in Malaysia. In his answer I sensed that he might have been drawing from his own experiences or the experiences of those close to him: "Young fresh graduates are often asked by their parents to join big firms and multinational corporations as a means to gain experience and capital in order to not start off as entrepreneurs. Working professionals who have been in a routine corporate job for a while find it very hard to leave to become entrepreneurs, as they are often discouraged by their spouses and family members and are many times earning well."

Whether in Malaysia or the United States, every entrepreneur risks failure. But in Malaysia, once one's family has achieved a certain level of success and stability—not an easy task for members of older generations—there is much at stake. The "honor" that well-established families in Malaysia have gained by surviving, thriving, and providing a good education for their children is not taken lightly.

One of my Chinese friends back in Cambridge comically described the favorite pastime of family gatherings in Asia: to gossip around the dinner table about the younger generation. Although my friend was generalizing, an image came to my mind of Mr. Lam and all the aspiring entrepreneurs in Malaysia at the "kids' table" beside their superiors, wondering if they would be talked about proudly or not.

The Rainmaker

On my final night in Kuala Lumpur, desperate to learn all I could in my waning hours, I let myself lose track of where I was—of the delightfully warm night, of the mosquitos nipping at my legs, of the mud squishing between my toes. I met Mr. Ng on a rainy evening at the beautiful Bayrocks Garden Waterfront Villas in Sunway South Quay.

The sound of pouring rain did not deter me from listening intently to Mr. Ng and his story of how he became one of Malaysia's legendary rainmakers.

In 1996, Mr. Ng returned from the United States after obtaining an MBA from the Wharton School of the University of Pennsylvania and a Master's in Electrical Engineering from MIT. Seeing the potential to bring America On-line to his country, he and a partner created "Malaysia On-line."

Although Mr. Ng had a family business to fall back on, there was definite pressure to succeed for reputation's sake. The choice to start a business that would enable Malaysians to connect to the internet seems obvious now. But with so few internet users in Malaysia in 1996, the decision then wasn't so clear. Mr. Ng knew he needed to explain, to educate, to have vision, and to be able to communicate his vision. But he also needed to learn what to actually do. Asking endless questions and seeking out myriad opinions from Kuala Lumpur to Hong Kong, he found a range of responses to his business concept, from intrigue to distaste. As he says, "When we started we had to meet anybody and everybody. We were also bold then, as there was nothing to lose in meeting people."

As Malcolm Gladwell points out in his *New Yorker* article "The Sure Thing," the successful entrepreneur "is often quite happy to put his reputation on the line in the pursuit of the sure thing." Mr. Ng was prepared to fail because he knew what that sure thing was. He saw the potential of the internet and of his business.

Still, Mr. Ng had no idea that four years later he would be able to sell his business, mol.com (at that time "Malaysia On-Line")—something he and his partner had started with $100—for $4 million, while at the same time they were able to keep the job-matching portion of the business. They were so motivated and confident in the business that they ploughed back 90 percent of the proceeds back into this remaining portion of the business.

This experience with mol.com propelled Mr. Ng into the world of entrepreneurship, from which he has not left. Keeping his customer base from mol.com, he started jobstreet.com, a company that has served as matchmaker for countless job-seekers and employers. It also offers services such as personalized websites on which candidates can showcase their skills, company insights, up-to-date salary information, corporate training materials, automatic job-type matching, and candidate notification. Jobstreet.com currently services over 200,000 corporate customers and ten million job-seekers. It has become Southeast Asia's leading online jobsite, winning recognition as one of the 200 Best Companies Under a Billion by Forbes Asia and KPMG's Shareholder Value Award. Recounting his experience, Mr. Ng wants his example to "encourage other entrepreneurs who have faith in their business to keep moving ahead."

There are real risks involved in entrepreneurship, but the wise entrepreneur is able to navigate through that risk. With persistent seeking and learning, he or she will ultimately create the opportunities that lead to success. Before anything else, however, all entrepreneurs need the passion to figure out what "white space" exists in the world, what problems need solving, what solutions will work, how those solutions can be marketed and deployed, and how they can be monetized. The never-ending cycle of learning motivates them.

Mr. Ng told me that in 2000, he had the audacity to approach the richest man in Hong Kong for advice. The story demonstrates why serial entrepreneurs exist: the thrill of conquering in one quest—and sometimes the failure of an initially promising endeavor—drives them to embark on another. The essence of entrepreneurship is that there is no manual available, no boss guiding you through your job, no roadmap to a million bucks.

Mentorship and Money

Covering the hills near the Sunway South Quay where I interviewed Mr. Ng are beautiful, lush rainforests. Later I learned that two thirds of Malaysia is covered in some of the world's oldest tropical rainforests, housing one of the richest ecosystems in the world. Entrepreneurship expert Mr. Daniel Isenberg says that an ecosystem is "the result of…hundreds of elements interacting in highly complex and idiosyncratic ways." I thought about Malaysia's entrepreneurial ecosystem, one that is growing but is not as old or as rich as Boston's or Silicon Valley's entrepreneurial jungles. If entrepreneurship is about learning, Malaysia's entrepreneurial ecosystem needs elements that will actually enable its aspiring entrepreneurs to learn.

A critical element of figuring out the "sure thing" is access to others who have gone before you, who know what you are facing and have conquered those challenges. No matter how persistent you are, not everyone can get the chance to accost billionaires in Hong Kong for advice. What aspiring entrepreneurs need is a community, one that will eventually grow to become an entire ecosystem.

At the Harvard Business School (HBS), there is an implicit assumption that everyone around you is very capable and interested in what you have to say. This social capital facilitates the opening of discussion because students feel their ideas will be well received and thoughtfully considered. The Boston area offers numerous mentors in the startup industry, people excited to have others follow in their footsteps. They not only provide advice but are looking for opportunities to get involved in promising new ideas and to invest in them.

In Malaysia, I was introduced to a third entrepreneur, Mr. Leow, from whom I gained further insight into the country's entrepreneurial ecosystem. After a few years at the management consulting firm Bain and Company, Mr. Leow jumped headfirst into full-time entrepreneurship. He is developing GuruApp, a knowledge-sharing, mentoring platform for high school students, one that he hopes will self-perpetuate and go viral.

The year that Mr. Leow has spent in Malaysia after returning from the U.K. has given him perspective on his country's startup environment. He lamented the lack of entrepreneurs, as well as the closed nature of the community: "Certainly the startup ecosystem is less mature than Singapore or Silicon Valley. There is a limited history or track record and no critical mass of successful entrepreneurs." As a result, "mentorship is…difficult to find right now. There certainly are several people who have built major companies worth between $40 and $500 million, but they tend to keep a low profile. Therefore finding mentors is generally limited to alumni organizations, Toastmasters, and the few small incubator programs."

Besides mentorship, a healthy entrepreneurial ecosystem must have systematic ways to access investors, legal advice, technical support, regulation information, and product design labs. At the Harvard Innovation Lab, or "iLab," which is located on the HBS campus, there are workrooms in which to build prototypes, workstations with whiteboards in which to hold meetings, a kitchen with free food, and even a large-screen TV with an Xbox. This place is open to the entire Harvard community, and its purpose is to make entrepreneurship a lifestyle.

The iLab brings in investors to talk about funding, lawyers to talk about legal issues in starting a business, industry experts to talk about regulatory issues, successful entrepreneurs to talk about challenges in specific fields, and marketing experts to teach budding entrepreneurs how to market and professionalize ideas.

Malaysia has started to work on a few of these fronts, including one of the most critical pieces — access to funding. Twenty years ago, venture-capital funding was scarce to the point of being unheard of in Malaysia, and entrepreneurs like Mr. Ng were often forced to go to Singapore to look for funding. Even now it can be difficult to find private investors or venture capitalists, except through organized startup community sessions. Recently, however, the government has started providing funding access and tax incentives, through special programs such as MSC Malaysia.

As Mr. Leow considers his options for Guru-App, he is aware of the progress Malaysia has made when compared to the environment in which Mr. Ng was forced to do business: "As long as you have a concept and team, it is relatively easy to get some amount of funding at the early stages by applying to government programs. There are different grants, and some will give up to $100,000 USD."

Over the past two decades, the changes instituted by both the Malaysian government and the country's entrepreneurs have significantly improved the startup ecosystem in Malaysia. The process of creating a startup is becoming easier. But there is still a long way to go.

Driving Change in Education

Sadly, nearly every Malaysian I spoke with complains of Malaysia's low educational standards. It is also unfortunate that seemingly every person perceived as "competent" had studied abroad. It is no coincidence that Mr. Ng, Mr. Leow, and Mr. Lam studied in the U.S., the U.K., and Australia, respectively.

One friend compared his experiences after moving from Malaysia to Australia for university: "I found that the level of discussion, the rigor of the classes, and what was expected from students was challenging for me.... I went to a pretty good public high school, and I come from a background where critical thinking is something that was emphasized in my family. But even with this strong foundation in a Malaysian setting, I still found it very challenging when I went to Australia.... The experience of the typical Malaysian student would be even more so."

Critical thinking and creativity in education were constant themes of the Trek. Among the cities we visited—Shanghai, Hong Kong, Singapore, Kuala Lumpur, and Seoul—Kuala Lumpur's education unmistakably lagged behind.

Malaysia's current model of education is lacking, as it does not develop the creative and innovative thinking necessary to support the country's entrepreneurial base. If an entrepreneur wanted to start a business in the 21st century that could compete globally, he would probably not choose to base it in Malaysia because he would have to import talent as the business expanded. To build an entrepreneurial base, one first needs the leaders themselves, skilled people who can think about solving problems. They need the wisdom to understand what the problems are, what potential solutions exist, and how to pursue them. Secondly, even if one is a skilled entrepreneur, one needs collaborators who can support one's business. Neither of these requirements is easily or reliably available in Malaysia.

Despite these issues, however, it was in Kuala Lumpur that I found the most frank recognition of entrepreneurial problems. Strikingly, among all the countries I visited on this Trek, Malaysia provided me with the most opportunities to meet individuals who were highly motivated to improve education in their country: the administration at Sunway University, young leaders at social enterprises like Teach for Malaysia, opposition party members, journalists, even students. Mr. Lam told me that pedagogical reform is strongly supported by the Ministry of Education, a critical element of success given that federal ownership of the education system will mean more consistency, easier benchmarking, and centralized performance management.

Crucially, Mr. Lam told me that school programs are beginning to support aspiring entrepreneurs, though they lack a coherent structure: "From my own experience of having gone through the education system here up to high school, there are no solid continuous platforms or systems in place that would really drive or prepare aspiring entrepreneurs, both in high school and universities. There has been a bit of traction lately among the local universities here, including idea-tion workshops and business plan competitions, but what stops the momentum is the lack of post-event incentives, such as funding and support for most of these activities. Students join in for the sake of participation, but there is nothing afterwards that really stokes the fire or passion in them."

Given their recognition of the weaknesses of the country's system, it seems that Malaysia has the right people to drive change. There are significant obstacles to effecting that change, but it is happening from the ground up, driven by the people themselves.

A Microcosm of ASEAN

"I mean look at Malaysia… it's a disaster. I don't see how they can come out of this. They've become so racially polarized. The ethnic tensions there are incredible. It's amazing what is happening there. So I don't see how easily they can emerge… without some blood being spilled on the streets."

I may never fully understand the complex dynamics of race in Malaysia, but from an observer's viewpoint, I certainly see it keeping the country from fulfilling its potential. The above quotation, from a commentator I met in Singapore, reminded me that race was the main reason Singapore was separated from Malaysia. Malaysia's racial struggles have been further highlighted by Singapore's contrasting success in integrating diverse ethnic groups, as well as by its obvious economic success. Many educated Malays see the opportunities in Singapore and choose to work there instead of in their own country.

The lack of coherent identity caused by racial diversity can be a big obstacle for business. If I were an investor or a new entrepreneur launching a product that could reach a mass scale, I would have a few concerns about Malaysia. Never mind the basic differences like age or religion—I would have to decipher differing beliefs, cultural practices, and languages and find a commonality that spans these identities. Every iteration would take an enormous amount of time.

Yet the most enlightening comment that Mr. Leow made in my talk with him was that along with these seemingly obvious disadvantages come opportunities with big implications: "One of the huge benefits of Malaysia is the market… For me, Malaysia is perfect for pilot-tes-ting a product—there are enough people to get a decent customer sample size, but it is manageable enough to respond to the customer needs… Once the product is successfully iterated in Malaysia, scaling up to the rest of Southeast Asia will provide a huge customer market."

Malaysia has a diverse population, living within one country with one governing body and one regulatory and legal framework. This is not dissimilar to the structure of the Association of South East Asian Nations, or ASEAN. In many ways Malaysia is a microcosm of the world around it. So what might be a challenge is thus also an opportunity for Malaysian entrepreneurs, for successful businesses that can thrive in Malaysia will be well conditioned to prosper in the ASEAN Economic Community set to launch in 2015.

Mr. Leow also chooses to see Malaysia's proximity to Singapore as an advantage rather than a liability. As he says, Malaysia is "close enough to benefit from some of the learnings from Singapore, but the startup costs are lower in Malaysia, primarily due to lower rent, and the market is bigger for concept testing."

Returning to Frozen Massachusetts

On our 22-hour trip back to Boston, I pondered everything I had experienced while in Malaysia. During the Trek I had been posting updates to Facebook, and I noticed that my grandmother had commented on one of them. I thought about how much Facebook has changed my relationship with her: now, although geography may separate us, she is connected to my daily life in a very intimate way. Just three years ago, my communications with her were limited to phone calls, but now she can see nearly every day what I am doing, when I get a haircut, where I am traveling. She interacts with me simply by clicking "like" and commenting on my posts. Considering this, I was struck by the way my world has been changed by the entrepreneurs who created Facebook, and I wondered in what ways the entrepreneurs I had met in Malaysia would change their country, and even the world.

Entrepreneurship requires more than a great idea and some luck. It requires a great idea with an owner willing to put blood, sweat and tears into making that idea a reality. It requires a great idea that has been refined a thousand times by people who have the skills to make those changes and who teach themselves what the market needs. It requires a great idea that fits into the local ecosystem, the local regulatory environment, and the local market where the product is launched. Successful entrepreneurs have met all of these requirements. They are like perpetual phoenixes, rising from the ashes of failure and rejection time and time again. They are resilient, persistent, and passionate.

Entrepreneurs like Mr. Ng, Mr. Lam, and Mr. Leow are conducting their work in a relatively immature system. Although the environments in which entrepreneurs operate may be different in market size, culture, legal requirements, and available support, the flame of self-creation burns brightly in all of them. I wonder if the momentum of entrepreneurship in Malaysia will continue and if its citizens will continue to push for change and equality of opportunity, thus ensuring that all levels of citizenry are engaged in the spirit of entrepreneurship.

If the existing culture can be changed to encourage citizens to pursue these paths, to achieve personal empowerment and the economic elevation of one's self and one's family, then individual change will lead to national change. At the core of this shift will be a small but critical mass of change agents, those who have the power to define the opportunities for future generations.

| Chapter 10 |

The Desires and Frustrations of Young Asians

Paul Yoo

Ed.M., Harvard Graduate School of Education

● ● ●

A classic question in the art of negotiation or of engaging in any collaborative work is "What does the other person want?" In order to understand people, you have to look at their interests and motivations. Knowing people's desires and frustrations is a critical first step to understanding their character because these sentiments naturally influence many of the assumptions informing their thoughts and decisions

Having lived and worked in South Korea for several years, I was interested to see if there were parallels between the general character of young people in Korea and that of young people in other Asian societies. What are the desires and frustrations of the different groups? During the Asia Leadership Trek, I found that I could quickly connect with young people in Hong Kong, and so I began to explore this question in the context of Hong Kong.

Arriving in Hong Kong

Sara Minkara and I were the first to arrive at Wan Chai Station. Sara is Lebanese-American, a brilliant and blind mathematician. She is also a social entrepreneur who advocates for the blind in the Middle East. I had the pleasure of escorting her around Hong Kong that night. Since then, she has become a close friend.

We were meeting Ms. Athena Lam and two other Trekkers. Ms. Lam is the program manager of SOW Asia, a social impact investor and a co-organizer of the conference we were holding at the Hong Kong Polytechnic University. She had requested a meeting with the panelists and speakers. I was on the panel, and this meant that I would have to forgo sightseeing at the Peak, the much-talked-about tourist attraction of Hong Kong that offers a panoramic view of the city. After days of back-to-back meetings, you can imagine my frustration when I was asked to skip the Peak and attend yet another meeting.

When we met up with Ms. Lam and the two other Trekkers, we decided to go on an introductory walk-and-talk around the city before settling down at a café. This was an exciting plan for the two other Trekkers, who would be able to walk quickly and become one with the Asian pedestrian rush.

Sara and I trailed the others at a distance. We were left out of the conversation, but it turned out for the better. It was my first time escorting someone blind: my visual and auditory senses were heightened, and I could see and hear more than I would have otherwise. With her I could not walk aimlessly, which is my natural inclination—I had to be a more mindful pedestrian. As a result, I absorbed and appreciated the urban landscape, and certain sentiments of the young people in Hong Kong became more understandable.

Housing

I felt connected to this dense city of seven million people. Every block had clusters of high-rise buildings. For miles in every direction there were towers after towers, and with every passing block I felt engulfed by the architecture. It was dizzying, with the noise of traffic echoing in this open urban chamber.

In 2011, a quarter of a million of these apartments were reported to be uninhabited, a result of the rich buying too many housing units without bothering to rent them out. The unregulated market in Hong Kong has attracted many wealthy mainlanders in China to buy apartments in the city as a way to invest their money in property or to get their money offshore discreetly. The resulting inflation in housing prices has fostered resentment against the mainlanders.

Earlier that day, one of the student ambassadors who guided us around the city expressed his distaste with this situation. He was outraged that wealthy mainlanders were coming into Hong Kong and creating limited opportunities for locals. He said they were "taking up the spots."

Such caustic language is not uncommon to the native residents of Hong Kong. What must it feel like for a young Hong Kong intellectual to walk around this city, surrounded by a quarter of a million empty flats where money has been parked by the rich? The price of the average housing unit in 2012 was estimated to be about fifteen times the medium income, and buying a place is a daunting prospect for any young person in Hong Kong. With every passing year, the prospect of home-ownership has ebbed further away for Hong Kong youth, and the constricting economic prospects are sobering. Though home-ownership isn't typically an imminent concern for college students, it was clearly on the mind of our student guide, and certainly it is at the heart of many young workers' fears about the future. Unfortunately, the desire for home-ownership goes unfulfilled for many people.

Hongkies and Mainlanders

Our student guide characterized rich mainlanders as unfairly "taking" things in Hong Kong, including the already-limited "spots" in Hong Kong's prestigious universities. He noted that other students at the school had also observed this trend.

I asked ask how he and other locals nationally identify themselves.

He was quite clear in his position: distinctly "Hongkie."

"We are different from mainland China," he said. Although he was meek in his demeanor, I sensed a definite undercurrent of resentment. Another student ambassador from the same school had a peculiar reaction to his statement. Her head swayed and sank slightly, and her eyes blinked—quick and arrhythmic. It was the kind of timid surprise you express when you hear something controversial and are not sure how to respond. Raising an eyebrow, she gave him a quizzical look.

"Yeah, Hongkie," he responded verbally.

She was, I learned later, from mainland China. I don't know whether they knew each other's regional identity, but the awkward moment I had witnessed suggested the sensitivity of the issue. A poll in 2013 found that 55.8 percent of Hong Kong citizens in the eighteen to twenty-nine age group identified themselves with Hong Kong, as opposed to China. This is greater than the overall average of 38 percent. Exclusive identification with Hong Kong has increased over the years: there appears to have been a big shift in the Hongkies' sentiments.

It is not difficult to imagine that when Hong Kong was colonized by the British in the mid-1800s, Chinese people residing in Hong Kong desired to retain their identity as Chinese. Reluctantly, however, they submitted allegiance to the Queen, mostly by default. Over time, their old attachment to mainland China subsided; along with a political shift came an ideological shift, and eventually the natives of Hong Kong enjoyed great economic prosperity.

Thus Hong Kong became a very different place—a much coveted place of opportunity for the neighboring Chinese. Many immigrated to Hong Kong during its early years of economic growth from the 1950s to 1980s. A new identity emerged, as well as a wide-spread appreciation of a liberal political ideology. Yet this new identity was fraught with uncertainty because it came with a legal expiration date: the handover of Hong Kong from the U.K. to China eighteen years ago, in 1997, sparked what the media has sensationalized as an identity crisis in Hong Kong. Consequently, there is regular friction in the streets and subways between visiting mainlanders and resident Hongkies.

Though a desire to retain a Chinese identity naturally strong during the time of colonization, this sentiment faded over the course of the next two centuries. This does not mean that natives of Hong Kong now desire to return to the days of British colonial rule; rather they desire to keep their own ideology and way of life, which conflict with those of mainland China. The consequences of the handover for Hongkies continue to be rife with uncertainty. A young employee in the fashion industry of Hong Kong commented that there is great anxiety about whether the "core values" of Hongkies today will continue to be maintained under Beijing's governance. The unsettled atmosphere has intensified the disputes and resentment between the neighboring political entities. And with the vast majority of young Hongkies today identifying themselves with Hong Kong exclusively, this pursuit of a unique Hong Kong identity is expected to grow steadily more prominent.

Such a contentious topic could not be overlooked in our Trek meeting with Mr. Jasper Tsang, President of the Legislative Council of Hong Kong. He was very politically savvy in his choice of words. He repeatedly called mainlanders "our relatives in the mainland." The phrase suggests that mainlanders and Hongkies are "family" in the global sense of the word but that there is still some distance between them because of the long history of separation. He did not provide us with a policy solution or a direct answer to the disputes over housing inflation and the identity crisis. Instead, he simply sympathized with the citizens' pain.

Entrepreneurship in Hong Kong

Many thoughts about the Hongkie character arose in my mind as Sara and I continued our urban quasi-hike. Finally we reached our destination: a quiet, corner café hidden away on the second floor of a nondescript white building. We rejoined the others, squeezing around a table by a window that opened out onto another nondescript white building.

Ms. Lam briefed us on the social innovation landscape in Hong Kong. She is a sharp young Chinese Canadian who supports entrepreneurs in Hong Kong. She has extensive knowledge about her ecosystem, and I learned a great deal from her. Because Hong Kong is a dense city of 7 million, things can happen very quickly—"everyone knows everyone." But though that may sound like a recipe for rapid social innovation, there aren't enough investors.

A city of 7 million with its own regulations offers too small a market for heavy-weight investors. So the puzzle that remains is how to find ways to unlock resources from other sectors and funnel them into social enterprises. Ms. Lam feels personally determined to solve this problem. It is her great frustration, and she isn't alone.

The other hurdle blocking the way for social innovators is a lack of candid conversations, especially in public forums. Ms. Lam emphasized that people in Hong Kong often fear losing face at public events, and this fear inhibits dialogue. People are skilled at packaging their stories nicely, but young entrepreneurs rarely hear enough about the challenges they will need to overcome. Their inhibitions, trials, and errors are not openly addressed.

This is where we came in: to speak candidly at the forum in the Hong Kong Polytechnic University. We were requested to speak about lessons we've learned from the problems we've encountered.

"I Don't Know"

The next day, at the Hong Kong Polytechnic University, people flooded the hallways armed with crisp business cards and strong handshakes. Professors, students, professionals, and entrepreneurs mingled with the hope of connecting to others in this wide network. A series of workshops and talks ensued, and before long the forum reached its final agenda. The panelists were called onto the stage one by one. I sat by our moderator, Francis, in the white spotlight, facing an audience of young entrepreneurs and university students. I pondered what I should say and how I should say it—though this wasn't very useful because I tend to speak plainly and spontaneously. In the end I stuck to my usual style.

The moderator asked well-crafted but standard questions about our story, our moments of epiphany, and our core message. He then asked us one last question: "Where do you see yourself five years from now?" I was the first in line to respond. I remember my answer well only because of my surprise at how positively the audience reacted. "This is a very interesting question because...I don't know." I smiled. "But I think I'll know in six months."

When the audience heard "I don't know," they laughed and applauded, and part of my response was muffled. I had inadvertently caused amusement by breaking a social protocol. There is nothing enlightening about the three words "I don't know," but the audience was relieved by the candid confession. I later learned that this incident was what people at the forum remembered and appreciated most. Even months later, attendees and fellow Trekkers remembered my comment. Following the panel, several people approached me with redoubled interest.

The reaction to my comment revealed two things. One, in a society where people fear losing "face," humble sincerity is both appreciated and desired. I am better at dressing down than dressing up, even to a fault sometimes, and it happened to work out well in this instance. Two, Ms. Lam was right: people in Hong Kong really do desire candid conversations about what they've been struggling with, and my confession of uncertainty resonated with the audience.

One of our student leaders came to me near the end of our Hong Kong expedition to say thank you. She said that she had been "so relieved" to hear my answer to Francis' last question. She and I had talked often during the Trek's stay in Hong Kong, and over dim sum I had asked her and the other ambassadors what their plans were following graduation. She and the others comically hung their heads and squirmed in their seats. Awkwardly laughing at their own frustration, they said they didn't know what they wanted to do. The feelings of frustration and guilt they expressed are not always a result of the "Tiger Mom" phenomenon that seems ubiquitous in American writing about Asian parents. Even when parents don't push their children too hard, students can feel guilty about not knowing what they want. Their economic and career prospects can sometimes feel suffocating and can make an exploration of their genuine interests even more difficult.

Characterizing Young People in Hong Kong

Here are some sweeping generalizations that should be taken with a grain of salt: the thoughts of young people in Hong Kong are filled with desires and frustrations. They live with steady housing inflation, which adds a heavy economic burden to their lives. Such constraints and pressures make it extremely difficult for young people to explore what they want to do. Additionally, Hong Kong's small market make entrepreneurship a difficult field to enter, compounding the difficulty of embracing innovation.

Young people in Hong Kong do not desire to return to the colonial era, but neither do they want to be absorbed by the Chinese mainland. They wish to retain a new ideology with core values that are uniquely Hong Kongese, but there is a lot of uncertainty about whether those values will be able to withstand changes in governance.

Why Does it Resonate With Me?

"I don't know what I want to do," said a fourth year student at Yonsei University in South Korea. She hung her head and squirmed in her seat, laughing awkwardly. Her expression of frustration and guilt was the same one that I had seen on the faces of students in Hong Kong. We were sitting outside, talking in the hallway of the language school in Yonsei University before the Social Innovation Conference hosted by the Trek, and I couldn't help smiling at finding myself in this situation again.

College students in Korea get as squeamish as students in Hong Kong when they're asked what they want to do, and that includes students from the best colleges. Psychologist Jeffery Arnett characterizes this period of development "by change and exploration for most people, as they examine the life possibilities open to them and gradually arrive at more enduring choices in love, work, and worldview." However, such exploration is constrained by the economic pressures facing young people in South Korea and Hong Kong.

The students at Yonsei University will probably earn mid-range incomes, if not more. But even so, the rising price of housing in South Korea will strain their budget. The 2013 McKinsey Global Institute report, "Beyond Korean Style: Shaping a New Growth Formula," concluded that most young people have to borrow from first-tier, second-tier, and even third-tier banks to finance their mortgages. In effect, 70 percent of their assets are tied to housing. As a result, not all of them will be able to realize their aspiration for home-ownership, and yet it is a deeply rooted desire among people in Korea.

As in Hong Kong, it is difficult for young people in South Korea to become entrepreneurs. Korea has a similarly small market, and so entrepreneurs there also suffer from inadequate access to venture capital. They end up relying on bank loans, but Korean banks are conservative in how much money they lend out. Inadequate support from bankruptcy and intellectual property laws makes the entrepreneur's path risky and less lucrative than it might be. When the Trekkers visited the Blue House, South Korea's presidential palace, we met one of the presidential secretaries and discussed Korea's creative economic initiative of setting up innovation centers around the country. It is a valuable step forward, but young people are still waiting to see if an entrepreneurial ecosystem will develop as a result.

Why Does This Matter?

Familial burdens, the difficulties of home-ownership, and the pressure to know one's future goals in uncertain economic times: these are worries and constraints common to young people around the world, not just in Asia. How does one escape from the feeling of immobilization inspired by the apparent lack of opportunities in the larger world? Perhaps the first step is to admit to each other, "I don't know," and to find common ground from there.

Korean people refer to themselves as Korean, and Hong Kong people refer to themselves as Hongkie or Chinese. It is very unlikely that they would introduce themselves to foreigners by saying, "Hi, I'm Asian." This lumping together of "Asians" is really a Western concept. Asian countries are vastly different, and they see themselves as each uniquely distinguished. Being Korean-American, I naturally feel like a foreigner in other Asian countries. But the conversations that I had with young people evoked such familiar sentiments that it swept away much of the distance I had previously felt about Hong Kong.

A powerful connection is formed when one says, "I know what that feels like." I learned to empathize with people in Hong Kong. We shared similar frustrations and had similar desires. Their pain resonated with me, and because of that their strangeness diminished. We had suffered in the same way, and therefore we were able to understand each other.

Perhaps their uncertainty and resentment would also resonate with young people in other Asian countries in addition to Korea, or with different generations in different countries. Perhaps these sentiments are prevalent in more places than I realized. What are the desires and frustrations of young people in other Asian countries? Is my own understanding of the Hongkies' plight, not to mention their similarity with young people in South Korea, indicative of a latent pan-Asia-nism, the emotional unity of Asian people? That is far too ambitious for me to claim, but the young people in different Asian countries who are currently progressing into adulthood certainly seem to have a lot in common.

| Chapter 11 |

People-to-People Connections in a Transforming Asia

Zach Przystup

MALD, Tufts Fletcher School of Law and Diplomacy

● ●●

Takeoff

The intercom crackled. "This is your captain speaking. We were just about ready to go before one of the crew here noticed a problem. There appears to be a plastic shard stuck in one of the engines, so we're going to, ah…take a look at that. We'll keep you posted as we learn more."

Four screaming babies, three hours, two whiskeys, and one bad movie later, the captain's voice came over the intercom once again, affirming that there was in fact a plastic shard lodged in the engine, though he assured the passengers that it was "under regulation size." Somewhat less than reassured, I re-buckled my seatbelt and put my tray in the upright position. We were off.

Aside from my time on the tarmac, there wasn't much waiting around on Asia Leadership Trek. In three weeks, we visited four countries and one Special Administrative Region (SAR), held nearly seventy meetings, and put on three conferences, in Hong Kong, Kuala Lumpur, and Seoul.

People-to-People Connections

While my ears listened intently for the sound of rattling plastic in the engine as our plane traveled eastward to Shanghai, my thoughts drifted to the last time I had traveled to this part of the world. In 2009, I taught high school English through the Japan Exchange and Teaching Program (JET). I was sent out to a rural town in the Hiroshima prefecture, where I lived on a hillside overlooking the Seto Inland Sea. My mother is Japanese, but I wasn't raised speaking the language, so this was something of a roots trip for me. I realized on that trip how much I still had to learn about Japan, its culture, and my family there.

Every morning, on my way into work at Toyota High School, I walked by a massive, kanji-engraved stone at the school's entrance. One day I asked one of the English teachers, Igawa-sensei, what the characters meant. He paused for a moment and said, "If you are brilliant, hide it."

This slogan represented the polar opposite of my own academic and cultural upbringing in America: "If you are brilliant, show it." As Americans, we are taught from an early age not to be bashful about our knowledge or talents but to display them. For me, the stone outside the high school was a powerful example of how critical it is to understand the cultural frameworks in which you operate; without it you will be utterly lost, and many actions and practices simply won't make sense. In this case, I gained a firmer understanding of why it was so difficult to coax my students to speak up in class: they did not want to stand out.

Seated on the plane with the other Trekkers, I pulled up the flight map on the touch-screen monitor. We were a long way from Shanghai—at least the length of three more bad movies. My mind wandered back to the classroom, this time one at Tuft University's Fletcher School of Law and Diplomacy. Just three weeks earlier, I had finished a course there called "The Foreign Relations of Modern China." In it, we had discussed the Macartney mission of 1793, the first attempt by a Western European power to open up the China trade on a foundation of mutual equality. The Macartney mission sought to relax restrictions on commerce in order to expand the British Empire's trade, and to establish a British Embassy in Beijing so as to secure direct communication with the Emperor. The Qing rejected both requests; the mission was a complete failure.

The incident displayed cultural differences at the height of their powers to confound. For starters, the British assumed that court proceedings would follow European protocol, whereas the Qing assumed that the British would follow Chinese protocol. Each side presented the other with lavish, symbolic gifts, but neither side understood the meaning of these gifts, and both were left unimpressed. Macartney's refusal to kowtow to the Emperor snuffed out what little hope remained for a successful trip. As a result of cultural misunderstanding, the British and Chinese made disastrous first impressions, thus spoiling a golden opportunity to build a mutually beneficial relationship. More than two hundred years later, the Macartney Mission's central lesson endures: if we fail to learn about and understand one another, we hurt ourselves.

I looked again at the touch screen. The digital plane seemed to be frozen in place. I scrolled through the movie selections. Discouraged, I pulled out my Asia Trek folder and leafed through our agenda for the next three weeks. Shanghai, Hong Kong, Kuala Lumpur, Singapore, Seoul. As it happened, all of these stops turned out to be fascinating, but at the end of the Trek, two of them stood out. One is in the process of a dramatic transformation, and the other has already undergone that change.

Shanghai, China

China is big. This was the first thought that came to my mind as we cruised down the eight-lane Huaxia Elevated Road from Pudong International Airport to our hotel in downtown Shanghai. We passed hulking factories, towering apartment complexes, and buildings that stood like sentinels on either side of the highway. The scale of the place was awesome; it was as if everything—buildings, avenues, bridges—had been supersized to accommodate a slightly larger human race.

The impoverished China that Henry Kissinger entered in 1971, when he met with Zhou Enlai to resume the Sino-U.S. relationship, is now largely a relic of the past. Over the last three decades, China has experienced economic growth that has lifted millions out of poverty, expanded the middle class, and made China the world's second-largest economy. Together, these extraordinary changes have made China the U.S.'s largest strategic partner and competitor.

This is a tremendous accomplishment, but it hasn't come without costs. For me, the most evident — and visible — of these was the pollution. On our first day in the city, I saw but didn't really feel the smog. On day two, I saw it and began to feel it. By day three, the air was uncomfortable to breathe and I had developed a heavy feeling in my chest, as if something heavy had sunk to the bottom of my lungs and was weighing them down.

The smog was a constant topic of discussion among the people we visited, from Chinese media members to high school and university students. Perhaps that isn't too surprising; it is difficult to ignore something you see and feel everyday. One American journalist based in Shanghai mentioned the growing sense of frustration among many middle-class Chinese, who have worked hard to build better lives for themselves and their families but cannot even go outside without worrying about long-lasting damage to their health.

As China's skies become hazier, the costs of its pollution problem are growing clearer. Sixteen of the world's twenty most polluted cities are located in China. A 2013 study by the British medical journal Lancet found that air pollution in China contributed to 1.2 million premature deaths in 2010, and China's own Ministry of Water Resources gauged that about 300 million people rely on water that contains "harmful substances." Lung cancer rates are soaring, life expectancy is plummeting, and the demand for coal is rising.

One of the next steps for China's growth is to shift from an export-oriented to a demand-driven economy. In an effort to generate domestic consumer demand, China is undertaking a massive project of forced urbanization; over the next dozen years, it plans to move 250 million rural residents into newly constructed towns and cities. This will pose many challenges. Underlying them is the question of how integrating seventy percent of the country's population into city living (the current percentage is half that) will help Beijing accomplish its stated goal of drastically reducing pollution by 2017.

From our meetings and conversations in Shanghai, it is clear that for China, pollution and environmental degradation have become the giant panda in the room. The way in which Beijing reconciles its need for continued economic growth with its need for a healthier environment and a better quality of life for its citizens will play a large part in determining the trajectory of China's rise.

As former U.S. Ambassador to China Mr. Gary Locke discovered, the tasks of conducting official diplomacy and building people-to-people connections often overlap, making for a delicate dance. During his time as Ambassador, Mr. Locke was alternately censured and praised by the Chinese for bringing greater attention to China's pollution and other sensitive issues, including violations of human rights and the treatment of minorities in Xinjiang and Tibet. According to Chinese actor Sun Haiying, Mr. Locke's biggest contribution as Ambassador was "to tell the Chinese people what PM2.5 is" and to raise greater awareness about air-quality issues. According to the *China News Service*, he was "a yellow-skinned white-hearted banana man" who liked to "criticize indiscriminately Chinese domestic affairs." Ultimately, diplomacy is about breaking down barriers and advancing mutual interests and understanding—but this cannot always be done without ruffling feathers.

While in Shanghai, I had a chance to try my own hand at cultural diplomacy, and I was reminded as I did so of Mr. Locke's difficulties and achievements.

Fudan High School

As our bus pulled up, gangly teens huddled in groups of five or six outside the main gates to the school. Most were speaking in hushed, excited tones, interrupted by the occasional burst of loud and nervous laughter. We were counted off into our own groups of five and six and paired up with groups of Chinese students, who were to take us on a tour of campus. At first the students leading our group were visibly nervous, as they tested out their English in front of us and, perhaps more frighteningly for them, their classmates. More nervous laughter ensued as the boys poked fun at each other's attempts to introduce themselves. Once we had told them our names, noting that their English was excellent (it was) and our Chinese non-existent (it was), the students became much more comfortable, and we were able to build a strong rapport with them. By the time we entered the lobby of one of the main buildings, we were already posing for pictures together.

Established in 1950, Fudan High School, or officially "High School Affiliated to Fudan University," has an enrollment of 1,452 students from the greater Shanghai area. It is one of the best high schools in Shanghai and all of China, and about 25 percent of its students go on to attend the prestigious Fudan University, as well as universities in the United States, Japan, and Europe. In 2013, eighty-one of its students went on to study at universities outside of China.

The students we met were extremely impressive. In addition to speaking excellent English, they were outgoing, cheerful, and good-humored. As they took us around campus, showing us their expansive athletic fields ("But the air is very bad," one student lamented), their gymnasium, their library, and their computer lab, which was fully equipped with Mac desktops, we bantered back and forth about culture, sports, and classes. After walking into their table-tennis room, I picked up a paddle and challenged one of the students to an impromptu match—ping-pong diplomacy without the fanfare. We played three quick points; cheers and jeers erupted with each return or whiff.

All four of the boys were avid NBA fans, which they demonstrated by reeling off the names of their favorite players and assessing their teams' playoff chances. Since I am a basketball fan myself, we made a natural connection. When we entered the school gym, a shooting contest was unavoidable. We loosened our ties, took off our jackets, and shot a couple baskets to more cheers and jeers before scrambling to get back for a formal meeting with the principal.

Walking around the campus with the students, I was reminded of the beauty of cultural exchange. Prior to our meeting an hour before, we hadn't known a thing about each other. On one side were Chinese high school students, on the other graduate students from Harvard, MIT, and Fletcher, all ten to fifteen years their seniors. But looking at both groups as we talked and interacted, I could see that we were all genuinely interested and excited for the opportunity to meet and learn about each other.

Both the U.S. and Chinese governments should do all they can to encourage and expand cultural exchange programs that will foster understanding and appreciation between young Americans and young Chinese. I believe this is one of the most important policies either government can implement. Both countries and their people would benefit immeasurably from such a concerted initiative.

Creating people-to-people connections forces people not to think in abstractions, but rather in terms of individuals they know from the country in question. People-to-people connections also have important implications for official relations between governments. After all, governments don't make policy; people in governments make policy. The more we understand about one another, the more difficult it becomes to demonize one another, and the easier it becomes to work toward mutual benefits and gains. Often the American media paints China with broad strokes, indentifying it as a big, monolithic bloc seeking to displace the United States. But China is diverse and complex, with over one billion people and perspectives. By pursuing people-to-people ties, the young generation of Americans and Chinese can take their countries' relationship into their own hands and shape it into what they would like it to become.

As we prepared to go on to the Trek's next stop, a leadership panel at nearby Fudan University, I recalled an earlier meeting with Mr. Chen Qiwei, chief editor at *Xinmin Evening News*. At the conclusion of our roundtable discussion, we exchanged gifts—a Harvard mug for Mr. Chen and a *Xinmin* mug for us. Mr. Chen explained that although our governments may have their differences, ordinary Americans and Chinese can always reach out to one another. If we are to avoid Macartney-mission repeats and build a more stable, secure, and prosperous world, following Mr. Chen's advice is crucial.

Over the past decade, no topic in international relations has captured as much attention as China's rise. Governments, businesses, and academics speculate over whether China will integrate peacefully into the existing international system or seek to restructure that system according to its own rules. Others wonder if China will continue its remarkable ascent or if any number of domestic flashpoints will stunt its growth. China's transition is not yet complete. Indeed, the Chinese government's goal is to "join the middle rung of advanced nations as a prosperous, democratic, and modernized socialist country" by 2050, which is still many years in the future. Nevertheless, if our visit to Fudan High School is any indication, China has a promising future ahead of it.

Seoul, South Korea

South Korea has already undergone one of the most amazing transformations in history. Up until the late 1960s and early 1970s, it was poorer than North Korea. Yet today South Korea is the only country to transition successfully from being a major recipient to a major disburser of development assistance. Known as one of the four Asian tigers, along with Singapore, Hong Kong, and Taiwan, South Korea boasts the world's twelfth largest economy and a vibrant culture with increasing global influence, as exemplified by the moniker "hallyu," or Korean wave.

Just forty miles north of the bustling, neon-lit metropolis of Seoul, across the Demilitarized Zone (DMZ), lies the most isolated and repressive regime in the world. North Korea holds 200,000 of its people in brutal and extensive prison camps. It employs a hereditary caste system that controls access to employment, education, health care, housing, and even food based on perceived loyalty to the Kim regime. North Korea threatens global security—and holds its own people hostage—with its nuclear weapons program.

Between the two Koreas, there is a marked absence of exchange. People-to-people interactions are limited to infrequent and heavily monitored North-South family reunions, unsteady communication between government officials, and, on the covert end, intelligence gathering. In North Korea, the exchange of ideas or information through South Korean dramas and music or any other foreign media is punishable by prison or death. The stark contrast between the two Koreas magnifies the tension between them. Indeed, largely because South Korea has achieved so much and has so much to lose, its triumphant transformation is an impediment to reunification.

In Seoul, we had the opportunity to talk about this peninsular divide with South Korean government officials as well as North Korean defectors.

Reunification?

Over lunch with National Assembly representatives Dr. Jeong-Woo Kil and Mr. Jaeyoung Lee, we learned about North Korean policy from two sides of the political spectrum. The ruling Saenuri Party favors a more hardline approach towards Pyongyang, choosing to make aid contingent on better behavior, whereas the opposition Democratic United Party holds a more conciliatory position, stressing humanitarian aid and seeking avenues for cooperation. Despite their differences, both Kil and Lee noted that the parties share one similarity: neither wants war. For South Korea, war would mean sacrificing what the nation has built over the course of more than sixty years.

The following day, we boarded our bus on a frigid morning for a trip to the DMZ. As we drove through Seoul, passing highways, traffic jams, skyscrapers, and bridges—all the conveniences and inconveniences of modern life—I was struck by the reality confronting South Korea. It faces an existential threat ninety minutes away from its capital city. Only a select few of North Korea's estimated twenty-two million people have anything to lose, but fifteen million people in Seoul alone have everything to lose. Yet it is impossible to ignore the massive human suffering inflicted on the North Korean people just a short drive away from downtown Seoul. South Korea has completed an unparalleled rags-to-riches story, but its greatness as a nation will not be fulfilled until the Korean peninsula is unified and whole again.

In early 2014, President Park called unification a "jackpot" for the Korean economy in her New Year's address, framing it as an eventual economic win for the South. But most people in South Korea are doubtful. Despite it being an explicit goal of the government, most South Koreans, particularly the young, are too fearful of the costs of reunification—which could run to hundreds of trillions of dollars—to support concrete actions that will make it happen. It seems that South Korea is moving too fast to accept the costs of slowing down. At present, the result of these conflicting feelings seems to be a distant hope, but not an immediate desire, for reunification.

Information Exchange

In addition to our trip to the DMZ, we had the opportunity to meet people who had crossed it. Mr. Ahn and Mr. Choi from the North Korea Strategy Group (NKSG) were kind enough to meet with us to discuss their organization's work, as well as their deeply personal and harrowing stories.

Due to his father's high standing in the Korean Worker's Party (KWP), Mr. Ahn held a job as a prison guard at Camp 22. At the camp, the guards were told that all the prisoners had committed unspeakable crimes, thus justifying their sub-human treatment. After a couple years as a guard, Mr. Ahn became a driver at the camp, which meant that he began to have more interaction with the prisoners. Naturally, he began to ask them why they were in the camp. It soon became apparent that the prisoners had no idea about the reasons for their imprisonment—most of the time, they were simply picked up in the middle of the night without explanation. This discovery ran directly counter to what Mr. Ahn had been told. The rest of the dominoes began to fall in short order. During a widespread famine in the 1990s, Mr. Ahn's father made a remark against the government, and his family was put under close surveillance. At this point, Mr. Ahn fully recognized the unfairness of life in North Korea and decided to escape by swimming across the Tumen River.

Mr. Choi was a dentist in North Korea. During that same famine, he saw people starving to death all around him. His calculation was simple: leave or starve. Mr. Choi first escaped to China, but due to the constant threat of being captured and sent back to North Korea, he decided to make his way onward to Mongolia. On his way there, Mr. Choi was captured and sent back to North Korea, where he was imprisoned for six months before being released. "Freedom is like a drug," Mr. Choi told us. Upon his release, he immediately sought to escape again through the same China–Mongolia–South Korea route. This time, he made it.

North Korea is still the most closed country in the world, but over the past two decades a steady trickle of outside information has begun to create tangible changes in its society. Growing access to foreign radio broadcasts, South Korean DVDs, and other media devices is changing the North Koreans' thoughts and attitudes about both the outside world and—more importantly—their own country.

Interestingly, both Mr. Ahn and Mr. Choi mentioned the role of foreign media, especially CDs, in enabling them to form a picture of the outside world. They noted that increasingly, this media is coming in digital form, such as USB sticks that are being smuggled into the country and contain South Korean movies and TV dramas. Significantly, this means that North Koreans can now see and not just hear about the outside world. The external media poses an existential threat to the regime. As Mr. Ahn and Mr. Choi noted, nine out of ten defectors have seen such DVDs. In response, the North Korean regime has used public executions to punish those who possess or distribute foreign media and to send a message to the wider population about the consequences of smuggling such media into the country. As with most things in North Korea, it is unclear if this has been an effective deterrent.

The NKSG presentation suggested that one low-risk, high-reward action the United States and other governments can take to help the North Korea people is to increase the flow of outside information into the country.

Reports from the U.S. State Department and two prominent North Korea scholars, Mr. Stephan Haggard and Mr. Marcus Noland, found that for North Koreans, consumption of foreign media leads to more negative assessments of their regime and its intentions, as well as to positive beliefs and attitudes about South Korea and the U.S. When you consider that North Koreans are bombarded with anti-U.S. and South Korea propaganda from birth, this is a very significant finding.

If North Koreans' exposure to foreign media increases, it is reasonable to predict that the North Korean regime will increasingly lose credibility. Once a critical mass of North Koreans is sufficiently informed and empowered, the regime could face a momentous decision. On the one hand, it could start to implement political and economic reforms. On the other, it could stage a violent crackdown on its own people. The former would be a step in the right direction, while the latter would call the world's attention to North Korea in unprecedented fashion. For the first time, the Kim regime would face mounting domestic and international pressure to reform.

In his book *Escape from Camp 14*, author Blaine Harden recounts Mr. Shin Dong-Hyuk's escape from one of North Korea's most notorious prison camps. Mr. Shin endures almost unspeakable suffering at the camp, but the driving force behind his decision to escape is simple: he is sustained by the prospect of eating grilled meat. We never know what information will be the tipping point for a person, community, or nation. We do know that providing any information at all increases the chances that the tipping point will be reached. For the people of North Korea, that moment cannot come soon enough.

In sharing their stories, Mr. Ahn and Mr. Choi are doing critical work. Such exchanges of information about conditions of life in North Korea and its gross violations of human rights will help to build empathy among South Koreans. This, in turn, will make it increasingly difficult for them to overlook the plight of their fellow Koreans. After years of living in South Korea, Mr. Ahn mentioned that he is "still shocked that forty miles from here, there are people with no concept of freedom whatsoever." Increasing the flow of information into North Korea could help to change this reality.

In its sparse coverage of North Korea, our media usually focuses on its latest nuclear test, the wackiness of its personality cult, or the travels and travails of Dennis Rodman. Mr. Ahn and Mr. Choi reminded us that the people of North Korea are what really matter. In doing so, they once again demonstrated the power of people-to-people connections.

Conclusion

As I boarded our return flight from Shanghai to Boston, I settled into my seat and heaved a sigh. It had been an exhausting and exhilarating three weeks. Fragments of images, thoughts, and experiences from the Trek whirred through my tired brain. I grasped at two that have stayed with me since the end of our journey: transformation and people-to-people connections.

China is in the middle of an astonishing transformation. Its rapid rise is causing a significant amount of anxiety among its regional neighbors and the U.S. That is why the increase of people-to-people connections between Chinese and Americans is so critical; such initiatives will help to build mutual understanding in an environment currently characterized by mutual suspicion and uncertainty.

South Korea has already undergone one astonishing transformation, but its evolution is not complete either. On the Korean peninsula, the exchange of information may lead to significant changes in both North Korea itself and the attitudes of South Koreans. If it helps to produce gradual, steady change in North Korea, the prospect of reunification may start to take root from the ground up. In that case, the Korean Peninsula could undergo its most radical transformation yet.

Throughout the Trek, our readings, discussions, meetings, and presentations facilitated my learning about these issues. However, my greatest insights came from people-to-people connections.

I was impressed by the students we met at Fudan High School in Shanghai—their knowledge of American culture and their language skills were both excellent. Recently, I learned that more Chinese students study abroad annually in the U.S. than the total annual number of American students who study abroad around the world. Although the students at Fudan High School constitute only a small and privileged sample size, I am doubtful that their equivalents in the U.S. are as knowledgeable and skilled in Chinese culture and language. As the U.S.-China relationship continues to grow in importance—and already it is the most important bilateral relationship in the world—it will be imperative for Americans and Chinese to grow in mutual understanding and respect for one another.

I was humbled by our meeting with Mr. Ahn and Mr. Choi at the North Korea Strategy Center. Their testimony opened my eyes to the immense human suffering that takes place every day in North Korea and to the failure of the international community to alleviate it. In this case, people-to-people connections between North and South Koreans, as well as among people around the world, will be needed to build the knowledge and empathy needed to support policies that will improve the lives of ordinary North Koreans. The arena of foreign policy is usually dominated by talk of national interests, credibility, power, and prestige. In the end, however, foreign policy affects individuals. There are few in greater need than the twenty-four million living in North Korea.

As I buckled my seatbelt and put my tray table in the upright position, the plane's intercom crackled: "This is your captain speaking…" Reflexively, I braced for the worst. "We have clear skies and temperatures in the mid-fifties, and we will be taking off in the next ten to fifteen minutes. Enjoy your flight, and we'll be coming around with our drink service shortly." No plastic shards. Grateful for this and for the amazing learning experience that the Asia Trek had given me, I closed my eyes. Once again, we were off.

Chapter 12

Asia at the Crossroads:
Avoiding Stagnation and Meeting New Challenges

Lars Ragnar Aalerud Hansen

MA, Tufts Fletcher School of Law and Diplomacy

● ● ●

When you go back to graduate school after years of full-time employment, one of the things you appreciate most is the array of opportunities it offers you, the regained ability to spot an opening and say, "Yes, I want to do that." This is what happened to me in the fall of 2013, when I received an e-mail about an information session for the upcoming Asia Leadership Trek. With a long winter break ahead and few firm plans, the Trek seemed like the perfect opportunity to do something that would be both fun and valuable as a learning experience. I jumped at the opportunity.

By the time our Trek started I had built up considerable expectations. The program looked great. I had met my fellow Trekkers, and they seemed both friendly and interesting. Escaping the hard winter I would find in both Boston and Norway, my home country, was an added bonus. So it was with only limited self-pity that I tweeted a complaint about flying on New Year's Eve as I boarded our flight from Toronto to Shanghai. The plane would quite literally not arrive until next year.

The New Year got off to a wonderful start. Having collected my baggage and later my thoughts in Shanghai, I could start to appreciate just how much the city had changed since I first came there. My previous visit to Shanghai had been in early 2001. At that time, Pudong Airport was brand new and the Pudong financial district was a ghost town of new, fancy, but entirely empty buildings. I recall walking along the streets among the rising skyscrapers and seeing an old, bearded man pulling his cart along the road. There was nothing special in the sight except that he had the road's six lanes all to himself. The place seemed desolate, and I remember thinking that it would never become anything like the images plastered in front of the building sites.

Wow, was I wrong. Seeing the bustling streets and sprawling businesses in the same area on the Trek not only drove home just how mistaken I had been; it was a vibrant physical reminder of what the Asian miracle really is.

For the transformation that has taken place in Asia during the past thirty years is nothing short of miraculous. Reading about more than 10 percent annualized economic growth is one thing. Seeing its impact in practice is quite another. This time around, Shanghai was to me, first and foremost, overwhelming. The scale of redevelopment is so grand that it can be hard to grasp. The apparent rise of wealth, as seen in innumerable luxury brand stores and giant cars, is astonishing. The sheer size of the city has gone from being already staggering at the time of my first visit to nothing short of mind-blowing today.

Yet, sadly, the challenges that accompany this modernization are on an equally grand scale: the pollution in the Shanghai area is overpowering, and it begs the question of what now? Many commentators have argued that the city's development cannot be sustained on its current pattern. It has already become a truism outside the country that China's model of development as a whole must be changed, and, judging by my encounters with Shanghai residents during the Trek, I believe this fact is now acknowledged in China.

If China's methods of development cannot continue, what does the future hold for the country? If it is approaching, as I think, a fork in the road, where does the road lead from here? These are the main questions I was left with after the Asia Leadership Trek, and the following chapter is my attempt to providing at least the beginning of an answer.

Before I continue, I should be clear about my credentials, or lack thereof. I am no expert on Asia, and a three-week study trip, no matter how thorough and well-planned, is hardly enough experience from which to draw wide-ranging conclusions. I write this piece, however, in the belief that the views of an outsider, no matter how raw his observations or unrefined his analysis, can help shed light on what will be a determining factor in the future state of the world.

For make no mistake: Asia matters more than ever, and its development will have a great impact far beyond the region itself. Asia is also a place of interest now for more people than ever before. Not long ago, Asian affairs were seen in Norway as the purview of a small group of specialists. This is not so any more—with the continuing globalization of Asian affairs, what happens there now affects the lives of people across the globe. And so our knowledge and understanding of Asia will become ever more important. In fact this was one of my main reasons for going on the Asia Trek in the first place: an understanding of Asia will be necessary for me even if I end up working on non-Asian affairs. Asia is no longer for specialists only; some knowledge of the region will soon be expected from generalists as well.

Similarities Transcending Differences

The Asia Leadership Trek took me not only to Shanghai but to four other destinations across Asia: Hong Kong, Singapore, Kuala Lumpur, and Seoul. Traveling from one city to another was a useful reminder of how different Asian countries are from one another. All are fascinating and unique. The sub-tropical climate of Hong Kong is a stark contrast to the freezing Seoul, and the almost supernatural orderliness of Singapore ends once you walk across the border to Malaysia. Strikingly, both China and Korea remain deeply rooted in Confucianism, while Malaysia is predominantly Muslim. Another dramatic difference exists between China and Korea and those countries that were once under colonial rule — Malaysia, Singapore and Hong Kong. Traces of their colonial eras live on in a range of institutions, some of which are the envy of other countries.

But despite all these important differences, I would argue that all the Asian countries we visited currently share one common trait: they have all exhausted the potential of the policies that brought the Asian miracle into being, and they all face difficult choices as a result.

In Shanghai, the environmental situation has arrived at a point where it can no longer be ignored. The Chinese authorities seem to have recognized this, but the depth of their realization and their ability to alter their course are not yet clear. I have never experienced anywhere else the degree to which environmental problems preoccupied the city; they literally seemed to be the number one issue on everyone's mind. Maybe, indeed, this preoccupation will serve to jumpstart a change in the city's policies. But, though the gravity of the situation is sinking in, none of our interlocutors seemed able to predict or formulate a policy shift that would be an effective response to this immense challenge.

On a macro level, it seems the Chinese government will have to shift its focus away from further industrialization and towards more sustainable growth. But this will probably have a negative impact on the country's growth rates, which are already slowing significantly, and several of the people we spoke with suggested that the authorities might become weary of social unrest if they are unable to meet expectations for further growth and rising living standards. Another argument we encountered that struck a chord with me concerns the fabric of Chinese society. As one observer put it, few Chinese know their neighbors these days. The unprecedented internal migration and urbanization has fragmented Chinese society, and this fragmentation makes it harder for the authorities to predict the social impact of new policies.

In Hong Kong, I was struck by the clear fragility of the current political arrangements. "One nation, two systems" sounds good as a slogan, but for it to be truly credible, both sides (in this case the pro- and anti-Beijing parties) must come together and find common ground. It is hard to see how a solution can be found that will satisfy the main actors in both Hong Kong and Beijing. But without such an agreement, the political stability that has been so beneficial to Hong Kong as a business hub will be in jeopardy, and citizens of

Hong Kong will face the risk of their benevolent autocracy being replaced by one that many would argue is far less savory. Can the two sides overcome their differences and produce a vision for the future that is credible and promising to both sides? I do not know, but I feel that this is an important crossroads in Hong Kong's history.

In Singapore, the uncertainty is fuelled by what can best be described as fatigue. According to polls, Singaporeans are now as unhappy as Iraqis. How can this be, considering the fact that they live in one of the wealthiest countries in the world and enjoy a level of safety unimaginable to people living in Iraq? But growth in Singapore has been sluggish lately (in Asian terms, that is!), and the government has failed to convince voters that they have a substantive plan for overcoming this challenge. As one of our interlocutors put it, "The government has not changed; the people have."

And therein lies the problem. Singapore's very competent government has in the past been able to get away with its autocratic ways, in exchange for stable economic growth, an excellent education system, and increasing creature comforts. Now, however, Singaporeans are no longer willing to accept their part of this social compact because more and more of them believe that the government is failing to deliver on its side of the bargain. The pressure for change is thus getting ever stronger.

In Kuala Lumpur, even the sluggish growth of Singapore must seem like a blessing. The notion that Malaysia has gotten stuck in the middle-income trap appears to be accepted as fact by a large percentage of its people. According to many of the Malaysians we spoke to, stagnation has set in. The results of the last elections, which saw broad gains for the opposition despite the skewed political playing field, also suggest that the Malaysian people are hungry for change. Among the ordinary people we spoke with on the Trek, stories of corruption and cronyism were plentiful and were told with a mixture of acerbic wit and vitriolic contempt for those in power. Many of our interlocutors also spoke of a crisis of education, which they rightly saw as harmful to the longterm prospects for restoring the country's competitiveness and growth.

Seoul stood out from the other places we visited primarily on one account: in South Korea challenges to the current model of growth are much more openly admitted and discussed by the political leaders. Indeed, building a so-called creative economy is one of the central goals of President Park Geun-hye. In our talks, the officials we met with were widely cognizant of the need to bring about changes to restructure the economy and restore growth. However, despite their willingness to admit this need, they were less forthcoming in describing how these goals were to be reached. Moreover, while the political leaders of Korea appear to be open to the idea of reform, I am not sure that the populace shares this sentiment. The few encounters I had with Korean citizens suggest that most people there are still strongly attached to the existing societal model—an unsurprising fact, considering that the country escaped from abject poverty as recently as the early 1970s and has climbed upward to rank as one of the world's most highly developed economies today. The hardships of the country's past are still vivid in Koreans' collective memory, not to mention the sacrifices that have been made to blaze their trail towards progress. Koreans are not eager to risk the benefits they have gained from these sacrifices by shifting to a new model of growth.

The Audacity of Diversity

When we asked what will be needed to combat the many challenges to economic growth and stability, people in all five cities gave answers that were surprisingly similar: one way or another, the countries in question need to become more innovative. While the degree of commitment to this concept and the depth of understanding about what it will entail varied greatly among our interlocutors, it is no exaggeration to say that "innovation" is becoming a buzzword in Asia.

At each of the conferences held by the Trek—in Hong Kong, Kuala Lumpur, and Seoul—I taught a workshop on diversity and leadership. This is a topic I consider of paramount importance in today's world. While its manifestation differs from one place to another, diversity is a fact of life in all societies if they wish to prosper and grow. And the only viable means for countries to sustain their diversity, in my opinion, is for them to improve their methods both of reaping its benefits and of mitigating its pitfalls. Diversity cannot be wished away, but depending on how it is managed it can be a source of either division or strength: countries that wish to grow must learn how to harness its power.

As a token of self-awareness and out of respect for my audience, I started every workshop that I led at our conferences by acknowledging that the audience was now facing yet another white European male preaching the virtues of diversity. Even in Europe, the combination stretches credulity. In countries with a history of European colonialism, it can easily be seen as bordering on offensive. Yet wherever we traveled through Asia, I met men in blue shirts and gray suits (usually with matching gray hair) preaching the virtues of innovation. If it is hard to imagine me—a white European male—as the face of diversity, I find it equally unlikely that these aging men represent the future of Asian innovation.

In trying to explain the great turnaround in Singapore after independence, one of the people we spoke with referred to the first generation of Singaporean leaders—Mr. Lee Kuan Yew and his peers—as "mavericks." I believe this description holds an insight of great value. The radical or even contrarian view of the outsider is often what is needed to accomplish a real break with the past.

This is precisely what happened in Singapore: in an age when import-substitution industrialization was the orthodoxy of development economics, the Singaporean leaders had the audacity to opt for an export-oriented, open-market economy. It is worth asking whether today's increasingly bureaucratic Singaporean government will have the same capacity for audacious policy-making. While these leaders are associated with competent and stable governance, it is important to remember that they were not the ones who started the Singaporean miracle.

This is also why I am reluctant to believe in the blessings of meritocracy as a model for Asian societies. Many believe that the meritocratic Singaporean model would be a better fit for China than Westernstyle democracy. I am clearly not in a position to dismiss this claim, but it is worth noting what our Singaporean interlocutor said: "The government has not changed; the people have." Could it not be that the Chinese people will change more quickly than its leaders?

Supporting the Innovators

I believe there is a link between diversity and innovation. Diversity spurs innovation because a diversity of perspectives is inevitably more likely to come up with different solutions than just one perspective. This is why, ultimately, I do not believe that aging men in gray suits will be the main innovators of tomorrow. Diversifying the decision-makers in society is one concrete way in which the countries we visited could spur innovation. When reformers make the case for increased diversity—when, for example, reformers in South Korea lobby to increase the proportion of women in the Korean work-force—they should remember that an increase in diversity is also good business sense—at least if the business is innovation.

But why focus on innovation in the first place? It is obvious that the innovative economy, if it may be so called, is a major asset for the United States. The value that top-end innovative industries provide is far greater than the value gained further down in the production chains. And as income levels go up in Asian countries, they will increasingly struggle to remain competitive in the fields of lower-end manufacturing.

The problem with innovation is that it is notoriously hard to bring about by fiat. A Korean parliamentarian told us that changing from a manufacturing economy to a creative economy is like shifting output from hardware to software. The change can be difficult because the advantages of "hardware"—material goods and specific laws and regu-lations—are so much easier to grasp. But, in my opinion, what really matters—and what holds far more to create longterm value—is the "software": the human mind.

What was the determining factor in the success of Silicon Valley? It was not the brilliant laws and tax exemptions that regulated the tech industry; in fact many American entrepreneurs decry what they see as government red tape hampering business innovation. In my opinion, what made the success of Silicon Valley possible were the people working there. At the risk of sounding unorthodox, I think the presence of a sufficient number of brilliant, rebellious, pot-smoking college dropouts who were willing to take risks was of much greater importance than California's tax code or its physical infrastructure. What California possessed was an environment where these mavericks were not ostracized but were instead given the necessary room to flourish and engage their creative energy. Therefore, while copying the infrastructure and studying the ecosystems of prospering tech industries is an alluring path for growing countries that wish to increase their levels of innovation, I believe it is unlikely to be sufficient to recreate these successes elsewhere.

Innovation will not come from men in gray suits. But currently our society, and Asian societies in particular, are geared towards producing more men in gray suits. South Korea, for example, remains a highly traditional society. While it has gone through unbelievable change and overcome staggering odds, the country's extraordinary economic transformation has not been matched in any comparable way by a modernization of social norms and practices. This is not surprising, as social change generally takes place at a slower pace than economic development. But to build truly innovative economies, I believe this area—social change—is exactly where Asian countries need to focus.

A Second Remaking of Asia?

I believe the Asian countries we visited have tremendous potential for growth in the future. They possess increasingly well-educated populations, their economies are fairly diverse, and the relative clout of Asia in the world will undoubtedly continue to rise. But I also believe that harnessing this potential fully will require a radically different model of development. And it is worth remembering, as I pointed out earlier, that the Asian economic miracle of the past half-century was initiated by just such deviations from the norm and by experiments with new policies.

What set off the first Asian economic miracle was a set of dramatic new policies designed by individuals who were willing to think out of the box. If Asian countries are to renew their promise for the future, I believe today's orthodoxies will also have to go; we have not yet seen the future, and I believe we have also not seen the policies that will bring it about. If the Asian miracle is to be repeated, the second transformation of Asia will have to be as radical and as consequential as the first has been.

In preparing for this transformative future, the focus of all Asian governments, not just South Korea's, should be shifted from hardware to software: investments should support and encourage the next generation by providing them with the best possible education, a necessary first step in the development of innovators. The importance of education in innovation is, of course, why education was such an important focus for our Trek. Today's educational methods will shape tomorrow's people. But despite impressive results in the Programme for International Student Assessment, I believe Asia's education systems are currently ill-suited to producing people capable of making the next great leap.

The countries we visited have built impressive manufacturing economies through strict adherence to discipline. But while Taylorist manufacturing requires rigor, innovation requires vigor. Asia's current education systems are adept at producing the people needed for the manufacturing, but they will not deliver innovators. To prepare for the future, these countries should remodel their education systems to foster the misfits and nurture the mavericks. They are the incipient innovators who can bring about the next transformation of Asia, and conformism ties their hands.

In order to harness the energy and creativity of the daredevils in society, changes to the education system are crucial, and changes to the structures of leadership are, I believe, no less important.

Trekking, Learning, Changing

"Young man, don't you confuse education with worldview." Several years ago I was thus reprimanded by an accomplished, elderly lady. I was a young diplomat, and she was the longstanding leader of an opposition party. I had just made the argument that surely, given the number of young people her country sent to study in Europe and the United States, the ideas they brought back would help build democracy in their own country. She had no faith in the argument. She was by no means opposed to it; she just did not think that a couple of years of exposure to a different culture would be sufficient to change ingrained values.

Today, being older and hopefully wiser, I agree with her. It takes time to change an individual's mindset. Achieving lasting cultural change takes even longer—and I believe this will hold true also in Asia. As one of my Chinese colleagues writes in this book, putting on a pair of jeans does not make her any less Chinese. It goes without saying that the skyscrapers of Shanghai have changed the appearance of the city, but a change of face is not necessarily a change of heart.

This is also why learning about Asia by going to Asia makes so much sense to me. Education should not be confused with world-view, but to develop one's worldview, practical experience is a much more powerful tool than knowledge gained from books. That is not to say that there is no place for books—they are crucial educational tools—but intellectual insight should be meshed with practical experience and personal reflection to produce a deeper understanding of and emotional connection to the topic in question. Discussions of a waning U.S. hegemony and the coming of Chinese power become both more nuanced and more substantive when their participants have all confronted the reality of China. Singapore is infinitely more complex than its garden-wonderland appearance, and one can only fully realize this by talking to its scholars and policymakers on the spot.

Asia will, of course, continue to change, but what this change will look like remains to be seen. I believe there is a huge potential role for indigenous, Asian innovation to play in the next round of renewal. But nurturing this innovation will require real leadership. The predecessors of the current Asian leaders were mavericks who did not worry about public opinion and the next election cycle, and the result was the Asian miracle. But they were also autocratic rulers who did not have to justify their policies to a critical electorate. Today all Asian countries except China are somewhere on the path towards democracy, and even though China remains a one-party state, public opinion has become vastly more important to its leaders. In all the countries we visited, the populations are more plugged-in and informed about world affairs than ever before.

Thus today's and tomorrow's leaders face a great communication challenge. This is clearly the case in South Korea, for example, a country with leaders who are more attuned to the need for policy change than their electorate. The people now demand a greater say, and so the Korean leaders face a steep uphill climb towards the creative economy they want to create. This change may ultimately become the biggest difference between the first Asian economic miracle of the past and the second miracle in the future: in the past Asia's transformation was imposed from the top down, whereas in the future Asia's leaders must allow for increasing bottom-up participation.

Allowing for increased public participation while at the same time enacting dramatic new policies will be a highly complex challenge for every country that attempts it, and it is by no means a certainty that all Asian countries will prove capable of succeeding. We in the rest of the world, however, must do our utmost to help them succeed. Sustained economic stagnation and rising social discontent in Asia would come with grave risks of great political instability, and in a globalized world, that would have repercussions far beyond Asia itself.

Many have said that the 21st century will be Asia's century. But what this Asian century will look like and how it will come about remains to be seen. The Asians themselves must embrace the challenges they now face in order to bring about this future.

Part 3

.
.

Epilogue

| Chapter 13 |

From Here
And On

Hungsoo S. Kim and John Lim

● ● ●

In July 2013, we began the five months of preparation needed for the January 2014 Asia Leadership Trek. After the three-week-long Trek itself, we spent another four months working with the other contributors to this book as they wrote and edited their chapters. It is now May 2014 in Cambridge, Massachusetts, and the polar vortexes of winter are finally being replaced with blue skies and sunshine. With the writing of this epilogue, we are officially at the end of our journey.

By the time you read these words, we will have completed the next Asia Leadership Trek in June 2014, which will include stops in six countries: Japan, South Korea, China, Myanmar, Thailand, and Indonesia. A new group of Trekkers, forty-two of them, will have embarked on their own unique journey of experiential learning and public service. The matchless energy that these Treks inspire in the participants and the learning, fun, and insights that they offer are what motivate us to continue pursuing new leadership initiatives in the heart of Asia.

In the midst of planning these Treks, we have considered numerous future initiatives that we hope to undertake. Each of them relies on the major components of our philosophical framework.

The Importance of Diversity in Comparative Analysis

In our work, we have come to realize the profound importance of embracing diversity in the learning process. Comparative analysis is richer when the samples are diverse, and this truth was demonstrated in several ways during the January 2014 Trek: we learned by engaging with leaders and laymen from all walks of life across Asia, in the public, private, education, and non-profit sectors. The Trekkers themselves contributed to the diversity of the experience, bringing different nationalities, career backgrounds, schools, interests, and points of view to our discussions.

One of the most striking features of the Trek was how dramatically the countries themselves differ from each other. Though each of the cities we visited was in Asia, they were as different from each other as Beijing is from New York or Seoul is from Paris. Yet the cities we visited all were relatively affluent; Kuala Lumpur is the outlier, but it still has a middle-income economy. In the June 2014 Trek, we are making a point of juxtaposing developed countries with developing countries, mature states with rising states, in order to give the Trekkers a more diverse experience of Asia's many facets.

We also realize that there are a wealth of insights to be discovered in lesser known countries. In future Treks, we hope to visit such countries as Cambodia, Mongolia, Bhutan, and Nepal, for we believe that these countries will offer invaluable insights into the development of Asian societies. Before we visited Yangon in 2012, for example, media reports suggesting that Myanmar would soon become "the next Asian tiger" distorted our views of the country. Our own experience of the country's poor infrastructure and sheer lack of goods and services, however, helped us to realize how much farther Myanmar has to go. As one professor at the University of Yangon commented, "Even North Korea is in a better state than we are." It was an eye-opening remark that helped us to understand the complex relative situations of different Asian nations. On the June 2014 Trek, we are looking forward to seeing how the situation in Myanmar has changed, two years later.

Finally, we were gratified to discover through the Trekkers' feedback how valuable this kind of experiential learning can be. We want to continue to help Trekkers gain sophisticated and nuanced views of the opportunities and challenges in multiple sectors across Asia.

Tailoring Our Work for Greater Impact

Because one of our central goals is public service, we are encouraged to see the great demand in Asia for knowledge and training in leadership. On the January 2014 Trek, however, we also saw the need to tailor our conferences more specifically for each country in order to maximize their impact. Although there is great value in introducing effective practices and ideas from the outside, the core of a great learning experience almost always arises from a strong internal understanding. In order to be better instructors and moderators, we need to increase our ability to ask the right questions, and we need to spend more time learning the local context for each workshop. Countries in Asia in the 21st century are trying to find the best possible methods of governance, models of education, and entrepreneurial ecosystems. There will be many challenges in achie-ving these goals, but in all of the societies in question, there are great opportunities for innovation and leadership. We want to help local communities identify and pursue those opportunities.

In accordance with this goal, we have strengthened our working relationships with our partners in Asia. We have also organized country seminars with experts from the Harvard community, who can provide insights on specific nations and advise us on our engagement with local communities. Our partners and faculty advisors will continue to play an advisory role as we seek to increase our positive impact on local Asian communities.

Following the Trek in June 2014, we plan to initiate a pilot project, the Asia Leadership Trek Fellowship Program, through which we will develop a structured instructional template for leadership training in various countries in 21st century Asia. Taking place in July and August 2014, the Fellowships will allow eight leadership scholars to travel through China, Korea, Malaysia, and India, focusing primarily on teaching at conferences and week-long workshops. These workshops will center on the themes of leadership and innovation, and we will, in addition, conduct inspirational talks, panel discussions, study groups, and mentoring sessions. The Fellowship Program will serve as an intensive platform to develop our understanding of the relevance of various leadership and innovation frameworks within the Asian context. It will also aid us in establishing our long-term initiatives for leadership in Asia.

A Center for Asia Leadership Initiatives

Through the Asia Leadership Trek, we are offering members of the Harvard, MIT, and Tufts communities the opportunity to learn and serve in a uniquely experiential way. At the same time, we are serving communities in Asia by offering platforms for meaningful discussion, training, and instruction. Ultimately we hope to develop a landmark, world-class program that will represent the best in Harvard training and use that skill and knowledge to engage other universities in Asia, America, and across the globe.

The Asia Leadership Trek has allowed us to surround ourselves with highly-skilled and like-minded people and to connect with organizations engaged in inspiring work. These individuals and organizations have played a key role in the project's overall success, and we will continue to rely on such collaborative partnerships in our leadership initiatives. We hope that in the years to come we will also work with many other innovative and open- minded individuals who are passionate about making a difference in Asia.

The natural next stage of our efforts to promote leadership training, educational innovation, leadership consulting, and public-service publishing is a Center that will support and institutionalize these initiatives. Already we have begun laying the groundwork for a Asia Leadership Institute that will provide the world's best leadership training, through both academic and cultural experiences. Within the Center, the Acumen Case Center will focus on research and courses on leadership that are based on the framework of "knowing, doing, and being."

The work of leadership is never easy. The challenges are immense, and the journey never goes as planned. But we firmly believe in the long-term perspective voiced by Mahatma Gandhi: "Learn as if you will live forever, live as if you will die tomorrow." May we live and learn to the fullest.

–Hungsoo S. Kim & John Lim
Cambridge, Massachusetts

| Editors' Acknowledgments |

●●●

We would like to express our gratitude to the many people who made the Asia Leadership Treks a reality:

Asia Leadership Trek 2014

To the January 2014 Trekkers themselves, with whom we spent an unforgettable time traveling, learning, working, and playing across Asia, in the process becoming lifelong friends: our co-organizer Nur Aziz, Saurabh Agarwal, Gil Alterovitz, Katherine Bragg, Joycelyn Eby, Carmen Flores, Sanya Gurnani, Anja Hohmann, Jennifer Jin, Anna Kneifel, Raymond Ko, Rachel Loh, Margaret McKenzie, Sara Minkara, Farzin Mirshahi, Roberto Patino, Neelam Pol, Zach Przystup, Cara Repasky, Irene Shao, Mark and Maria Syms, Fabian Toegel, Adam Turney, Keeran Sivarajah, Vidushi Tekriwal, Nikki Skovran, Daniel Wallance, Karol Mark Yee, Paul Yoo, and Zhoulai Zhu. We would like to especially recognize Lars Hansen who took up a leadership role in helping organize the authors and provide advice on early drafts.

To Abbey Onn, who supported us tirelessly at the Center for Public Leadership at the Harvard Kennedy School, believing in our idea and providing advice in our formative stages.

To the professors and instructors at the Harvard Kennedy School and Harvard Graduate School of Education who graciously offered their instruction, advice, and mentorship to the Asia Leadership Trek: Marie Danziger, Monica Higgins, Jorrit de Jeong, Jal Mehta, and Paul Reville.

To Greg Harris, for his advice and guidance on this book project, and helping us connect with Alex Green who shepherded this from manuscript form to a designed, finished book.

To the Teaching Fellows and expert practitioners who lent their time and talents in personalized workshops for this initiative: Barbara Hou, Nazanin Karimi, Michael Koehler, Christian Brei, Sarah Glavey, and Joeri van den Steenhoven.

We are especially thankful to the Harvard Kennedy School for providing us with a wonderful work space—namely the student lounge and the forum—where we brainstormed, discussed, and wrote this book. It provided us with an amazing environment in which we were filled with inspiration.

We are also indebted to individual supporters and partners of the Asia Leadership Trek, who played an invaluable role in organizing our program in various cities across Asia:

In Shanghai: Yingshi Bai, Qian Zhou, and Liang Cui at the China Young Leaders Foundation; the team at the New World Development Company; and Max Liu, Kelly Chen, and Feifan Huang from Project ConneXion; and Austin Volz.

Jeff Chen, practically a Trekker himself, deserves a special mention for taking a leadership role in arranging the logistics for both Shanghai and Hong Kong. Scarlett Yin and Janet Wong also played critical roles in arranging our programs in Shanghai and Hong Kong respectively.

In Hong Kong we enjoyed an informative tour of the city over the weekend thanks to student ambassadors from the local universities: Janet Wong, Andrew Lee, Hollie Chung, Emma Jiatong Wu, Zoe Fan, Ting Fung Chiu, Cindy Tam, Tsz Kit Zhuang, Ken Yung, Irisa Lam, and Ronald Huang. Wendy Yeung from the Office of the Legislative Council played an instrumental role in arranging our dialogue with Jasper Tsang.

We also had a wonderful time working with Athena Lam and Scott Lawson at SOW Asia, Gwen Chan from the Hong Kong Polytechnic University Jockey Club Design Institute for Social Innovation, and Paul Wang from the Hong Kong Polytechnic University Institute for Entrepreneurship. The social innovation forum we co-organized with these three is just one of the many public-service projects in which they are involved.

We would like to offer special thanks to Rachel Loh, one of our Trekkers and an author of one of the essays in this book, for her time and effort in organizing insightful meetings during our time in Singapore; as well as the Lee Kuan Yew School of Public Policy for their logistical support.

We are indebted to several individuals in Kuala Lumpur who are committed to public leadership in their country and who supported our conference at Sunway University: the legendary Dr. Jeffrey Cheah, founder and chairman of Sunway Group and founding trustee of Jeffrey Cheah Foundation, Dr. Elizabeth Lee and Ng Beng Lean from Sunway Education Group; UEM Group Berhad; Khazanah Nasional Berhad; and the teams at Teach for Malaysia and Bank Negara.

In Seoul, local university students arranged meetings and showed us around their city: Youhee Choi, Shinyoung Roh, Hannah Yang, Jung Hyun Kim, and Claire Hayn Lee. We also received immense support from Dr. Young Joon Mok and Minjo Kim from Kim & Chang; KilJeong-Woo and Lee Jaeyoung, the members of the National Assembly; Wonhoon Park, a former senior executive at the Korea Broadcasting Company; Youseek Choi from the Citibank Korea; Sunhong Min from Amore Pacific; CJ Entertainment; and Subae Yang from Korea Tourism Organization. We also extend gratitude to Daesik Kim from the Open Lab, who helped our group organize a great conference at Yonsei University.

We would like to thank Morgan McVicar, a lecturer at HKS, for the many hours he spent with us refining our abilities in writing and editing. We would also like to recognize Alexandria Marzano-Lesnevich, a lecturer at HKS, for actively advising us on this project and connecting us to the right people. Through her help, we were able to connect with Ursula DeYoung, our talented and speedy editor, who brought our book to its current polished state.

Asia Leadership Trek III

To the June 2014 Trekkers, with whom we spent an unforgettable time traveling, learning, working, and playing across Asia: Co-Organizers Jiro Yoshino, Andi Sparringa, Fuadi Pitsuwan, John Lim, Max Dengyang Liu and Wenhui Ren, and Trekkers Tommy Gallaway, Germaine Chua, Mitchell Ji, Kimberly Fernandes, Marina Chan, Anders Graugaard, Audrene Eloit, Saleh El Machnouk, Ayoub Eddaira, Ignacio Alvaro, Frederick Pierru, Mariana Ruiz Morales, Miguel Angel Santos, Michael Koehler, Juan Pablo Remolina, Thomas Favennec, Hector Escamilla, Antara Lahiri, Christian Brei, Sarah Glavey, Kawtar Eddahmani, Ahmed Eddahmani, Shazia Khan, Stephanie Oviedo, Karly Schledwitz, Jieun Baek, Parisa Roshan, Shimon Levy, Gauri Goyal, Valerie von der Tann, Tracey Hsu, John Lee, Zeina Shuhaibar, and Dafu Zhang.

To the Asia Center of Harvard University and the Ash Center of Democratic Governance and Innovation, which supported us, believed in our idea and provided advice in both our formative and our execution stages.

To the professors and staff at the Harvard University who graciously offered their instruction, advice, and mentorship to the Asia Leadership Trek: Dr. Arthur Kleinman, Dr. Jay Rosengard, Jon Mills, Tim Burke, Alison Barron, and Trisiawati Bantacut.

To Lam Kin Chung, our supporter and mentor, for his sponsorship.

To John Lim, for his work with the authors.

To Morgan McVicar, for his advice and guidance.

To the Teaching Fellows and expert practitioners, Michael Koehler, Christian Brei and Sarah Glavey, who lent their time and talents in personalized workshops.

To the individual supporters and partners of the Asia Leadership

Trek, who played an invaluable role in organizing our program in various cities across Asia:

In Tokyo, Jiro Yoshino, Yasuhiro Ono, members of BizJapan, Ozawa Akihiro and Route H of Benesse Corporation.

In Seoul, senior executives at Samsung Group, Dr. Young Joon, Mok and Minjo Kim from Kim & Chang; Wonhoon Park, Amore Pacific, Subae Yang, Chung Ui-hwa, Park Jin, and Junhee.

In Beijing, Young China Leaders Foundation, Peter Bai, Joe Guan, and Wenhui Ren, Dengyang Liu, Gao Xiqing and Cao Yu of China Investment Bank, Dr. Huang Yiping, Dr. Xu Hongcai, Liu Xiaolin, Lei Zhang of Hillhouse Capital, Dr. Zhang Yunling and Dr. Yang Danzhi of the Chinese Academy for Social Sciences, Joy Ma and Jeff Chen, and Allen Liang.

In Yangon, Paradorn Kunkongkaphan and his staff at the MK Group, the Union of Myanmar Federation of Chambers of Commerce, the Myanmar Peace Center, the National League for Democracy, and the U.S. Embassy in Myanmar.

In Bangkok, Fuadi Pitsuan's mentors and friends, the Democrat Party, the RMA Group, *Bangkok Post*, TDRI, and the U.S. Embassy.

In Jakarta, Andi Sparringa, the Young Entrepreneurs Club of Indonesia, Lippo Group, John Riady and Soetikno of the MRA Group, Daniel Sparringa, Minister of Foreign Affairs Marty Natalegawa, and Minister of Tourism, Culture and Creative Economy Mari Elka Pangestu.

In Kuala Lumpur, Dr. Jeffrey Cheah, Dr. Lee Weng Keng, Dr. Elizabeth Lee, Ng Beng Lean from the Jeffrey Cheah Foundation and the Sunway Education Group.

In Pohang and Ansan, Vice-President, Shin-ik Kang, and Program

Coordinator, Daniel Kim, of the Handong Global Leadership Program, and Geumsoon Park, Ansan Program Coordinator.

Finally, we would like to thank our friends, our families, and our Maker, without whom our lives would not be filled with love, prayers, and new mercies every day.

| Appendix I |
Fellowship Itinerary

● ● ●

Asia Leadership Fellowship 2014

Date	Events
June 30 – July 4	**Asia Leadership Scholars Program** Leadership in a New Asia Beijing, China
July 7 – 11	**Asia Leadership Youth Camp** Leaders in Development Beijing, China
July 15 – 25	**Asia Leadership Youth Conference** Leading Change: Organizing and Action Ansan, Korea
July 28 – August 1	**Emerging Leaders Program for Youth** Leaders in Development Seoul, Korea
August 4 – 8	**Asia Leadership Summer School** Art and Practice of Leadership Development Seoul, Korea
August 11 – 15	**Asia Leadership Youth Camp** Art and Practice of Leadership Development Pohang, Korea
August 18 – 22	**Asia Leadership Camp** Leadership and Innovation in the 21st Century Kuala Lumpur, Malaysia

November 12 – 15	**Trilateral Leadership Summit I** Preparing for the Age of Asia Seoul, Korea
November 16	**Korea Leadership Conference** From Good Intention to Leading Social Change Seoul, Korea

| Appendix II |
List of Trekkers and Fellows

●●●

Asia Leadership Trek 2014

Adam Turney, *American*
Ed.M., Harvard Graduate School of Education

Anja Hohmann, *German*
MPP, Harvard Kennedy School of Government

Anna Kneifel, *German*
MTS, Harvard Divinity School

Cara Repasky, *American*
MBA, Harvard Business School

Carmen Flores, *American*
MBA, Harvard Business School

Daniel Wallance, *American*
MS, MIT Sloan School of Management

Fabian Togel, *German*
MPA, Harvard Kennedy School of Government

Farzin Mirshahi, *British*
MPP, Harvard Kennedy School of Government

Gil Alterovitz, *American*
Director of Biomedical Cybernetics Laboratory, Harvard Medical School

Hungsoo S. Kim, *Korean*
President, Center for Asia Leadership Initiatives
MPA, Harvard Kennedy School of Government

Irene Shao, *Canadian*
Ed.M., Harvard Graduate School of Education

Jennifer Jin, *American*
MBA, MIT Sloan School of Management

John Lim, *Canadian/Filipino*
Yonsei/Fletcher, Harvard Extension School

Joycelyn Eby, *American*
Ed.M., Harvard Graduate School of Education

Karol Mark Yee, *Filipino*
Ed.M., Harvard Graduate School of Education

Katherine Bragg, *British*
MBA, Harvard Business School

Keeran Sivarajah, *Malaysian*
Ed.M., Harvard Graduate School of Education

Lars Ragnar Aalerud Hansen, *Norwegian*
MA, Tufts Fletcher School of Law and Diplomacy

Margaret McKenzie, *American*
MALD, Tufts Fletcher School of Law and Diplomacy

Maria Syms, *American*
MPA, Harvard Kennedy School of Government

Mark Syms, *American*
Otologist/Neurotologist, Arizona Hearing Center

Neelam Pol, *Indian*
Ed.M., Harvard Graduate School of Education

Nikki Skovran, *American*
MBA, Harvard Business School

Nur Aziz, *Malaysian*
Ed.M., Harvard Graduate School of Education

Paul Yoo, *American*
Ed.M., Harvard Graduate School of Education

Rachel Loh, *Malaysian*
MPP, Harvard Kennedy School of Government

Raymond Ko, *Hongkonger*
PhD, Harvard University

Roberto Patino, *Venezuelan*
MPP, Harvard Kennedy School of Government

Sara Minkara, *American*
MPP, Harvard Kennedy School of Government

Sanya Gurnani, *Indian*
MBA, Harvard Business School

Saurabh Agarwal, *Indian*
MPP, Harvard Kennedy School of Government

Shazia Khan, *American/Pakistani*
Ed.M., Harvard Graduate School of Education

Vidushi Tekriwal, *British*
MBA, Harvard Business School

Zach Przystup, *American*
MALD, Tufts Fletcher School of Law and Diplomacy

Zhoulai Zhu, *Chinese*
Ed.M., Harvard Graduate School of Education

●●●

Asia Leadership Trek III

Ahmed Eddahmani, *Moroccan*
JD, Rabat Law School

Anders Graugaard, *Dane*
MPA, Harvard Kennedy School of Government

Andi Sparringa, *Indonesian*
MA, Tufts Fletcher School of Law and Diplomacy

Antara Lahiri, *Indian*
MPA, Harvard Kennedy School of Government

Audrene Eloit, *French*
MPA, Harvard Kennedy School of Government

Ayoub Eddaira, *Moroccan*
MPA, Harvard Kennedy School of Government

Christian Brei, *German*
MPA, Harvard Kennedy School of Government

Dafu Zhang, *Chinese*
MS, MIT Sloan School of Management

Erica Leinmiller, *American*
MPP, Harvard Kennedy School of Government

Frederick Pierru, *French*
MPA, Harvard Kennedy School of Government

Fuadi Pitsuwan, *Thai*
MPP, Harvard Kennedy School of Government

Gauri Goyal, *British*
MPP, Harvard Kennedy School of Government

Germaine Chua, *Singaporean*
MA, Harvard Graduate School of Arts and Sciences

Hector Escamilla, *Mexican*
MPA, Harvard Kennedy School of Government

Hungsoo S. Kim, *Korean*
President, Center for Asia Leadership Initiatives
MPA, Harvard Kennedy School of Government

Ignacio Alvaro, *Spaniard*
MPA, Harvard Kennedy School of Government

Jieun Baek, *American*
MPP, Harvard Kennedy School of Government

Jiro Yoshino, *Japanese*
MPA, Harvard Kennedy School of Government

John Lim, *Canadian/Filipino*
Yonsei/Fletcher, Harvard Extension School

Juan Pablo Remolina, *Colombian*
MPA, Harvard Kennedy School of Government

Karly Schledwitz, *American*
MPP, Harvard Kennedy School of Government

Kawtar Eddahmani, *French/Moroccan*
MPAID, Harvard Kennedy School of Government

Kim Fernandes, *Indian*
Ed.M., Harvard Graduate School of Education

Mariana Ruiz Morales, *Mexican*
BSc, Universidad La Salle

Marina Chan, *Hongkonger*
Ed.M., Harvard Graduate School of Education

Mark Dlugash, *American*
MPP, Harvard Kennedy School of Government

Michael Koehler, *German*
MPA, Harvard Kennedy School of Government

Miguel Santos, *Venezuelan*
MPA, Harvard Kennedy School of Government

Mitchell Ji, *American*
MBA, Harvard Business School

Parisa Roshan, *American/Iranian*
MPP, Harvard Kennedy School of Government

Saleh El Machnouk, *Lebanese*
MPA, Harvard Kennedy School of Government

Sarah Glavey, *Irish*
MPA, Harvard Kennedy School of Government

Shazia Khan, *American/Pakistani*
Ed.M., Harvard Graduate School of Education

Shimon Levy, *Israeli*
MPP, Harvard Kennedy School of Government

Stephanie Oviedo, *American/Puerto Rican*
MPP, Harvard Kennedy School of Government

Teresa Conrad, *German*
MPP, Harvard Kennedy School of Government

Thomas Favennec, *French*
MPA, Harvard Kennedy School of Government

Thomas Gallaway, *American*
MALD, Tufts Fletcher School of Law and Diplomacy

Tracey Hsu, *American*
MPP, Harvard Kennedy School of Government

Valerie von der Tann, *German*
MPP, Harvard Kennedy School of Government

Zeina Shuhaibar, *American/Lebanese*
MPA, Harvard Kennedy School of Government

●●●

Asia Leadership Fellowship Summer 2014

Andi Sparringa, *Indonesia*
MA, Tufts Fletcher School of Law and Diplomacy

April Bang, *Korean*
MPP, Harvard Kennedy School of Government

Eugene B. Kogan, *American*
Teaching Scholar, Harvard Kennedy School of Government

Hungsoo S. Kim, *Korean*
President, Center for Asia Leadership Initiatives
MPA, Harvard Kennedy School of Government

John Lim, *Canadian/Filipino*
Yonsei/Fletcher, Harvard Extension School

John Lee, *American*
MPA, Harvard Kennedy School of Government

Lance Li, *American*
MPP, Harvard Kennedy School of Government

Lauren Swersky, *American*
Ed.M., Harvard Graduate School of Education

Rajen Patel *Indian*
MPA Harvard Kennedy School of Government
MBA, Stanford Graduate School of Business

Shazia Khan, *American/Pakistani*
Ed.M., Harvard Graduate School of Education

●●●

Asia Leadership Fellowship November 2014

Anna Yoon, *American*
MBA, Harvard Business School

Hungsoo S. Kim, *Korean*
President, Center for Asia Leadership Initiatives
MPA, Harvard Kennedy School of Government

Kim Fernandes, *Indian*
Ed.M., Harvard Graduate School of Education

Jiro Yoshino, *Japanese*
MPA, Harvard Kennedy School of Governmen

John Lim, *Canadian/Filipino*
Yonsei/Fletcher, Harvard Extension School

John Lee, *American*
MPA, Harvard Kennedy School of Government

Marina Chan, *Hongkonger*
Ed.M., Harvard Graduate School of Education

Mitchell Ji, *American*
MBA, Harvard Business School

Pitichoke Chulapamornsri, *Thai*
MPP, Harvard Kennedy School of Government

Shazia Khan, *American/Pakistani*
Ed.M., Harvard Graduate School of Education

| Appendix III |
List of Conference Topics

●●●

Asia Leadership Conference

Workshop Topics

1. Addressing Cognitive Biases in Decision Making
2. Adaptive Leadership
3. Art of Communication
4. Authentic Leadership
5. Becoming a Better Decision Maker
6. Better Together: Empowering Effective Collaboration between Men and Women
7. Building a Public Narrative
8. Building Bridges through Inter-Cultural and Ethnic Dialogue
9. Campaigns 101: How to Run and Manage a Campaign
10. Creating and Claiming Value in Negotiations
11. Creating Inclusive Workplaces–Targeting and Minimizing Conflict
12. Creating Shared Value
13. Cross-Cultural Communication: Embracing Others and

Debunking Stereotypes

14. Decision Making
15. Design Thinking and Innovation
16. Designing a 21st Century Learning Environment
17. Disciplined Entrepreneurship
18. Effective Language Acquisition
19. Entrepreneurial Venture Evaluation
20. Entrepreneurship in Developing Countries
21. Financing Entrepreneurial Ventures
22. How to Give an Impromptu Speech
23. How to Lead High-Impact Meetings
24. How to Use Behavioural Insights to Become a Better Leader
25. Improving Performance and Outcomes in Negotiation
26. Influencing Techniques: How to be More Effective
27. Leadership and Identity
28. Leadership and Management
29. Leadership in Sustainable Urban Planning
30. Making of a Politician
31. Managing Innovation in the Cyber Age: Controlled Chaos
32. Measuring Performance of Non-Profits
33. Navigating Differences in Political Cultures
34. Negotiation Strategies for Managers
35. Overcoming Hidden Barriers to Change (Immunity to Change)
36. Persuasion: An Everyday Exercise to Rally Opinions
37. Political Organizing
38. Public Speaking and Media Training
39. Social Change Starts with Good Intentions

40. Social Entrepreneurship: From Idea to Realization
41. The Art of Effective Advocacy
42. The Reflective Leader
43. Transformational Leadership
44. Using Stories to Mobilize Change
45. Women and Leadership

Career Mentoring Topics

1. Applying to U.S. Universities: General
2. Applying to U.S. Universities: Finding and Choosing the Right Program
3. Applying to U.S. Universities: MBA, MPA or JD Programs
4. Career in Academics, Research and Think Tanks
5. Career in Advocacy and Campaigning
6. Career in Education
7. Career in Engineering-General
8. Career in Finance & Banking
9. Career in Foreign Service
10. Career in International Development & Aid
11. Career in Legal
12. Career in Marketing
13. Career in Management Consulting
14. Career in Medicine & Health
15. Career in Nonprofit
16. Career in Politics
17. Career in Social Entrepreneurship
18. Career in Sports

19. Leadership Coaching
20. Tech Start-ups

Professional Development Topics

1. All About Publishing Your Own Book
2. Building a Personal Branding
3. Building Resume
4. Creative Writing
5. Developing a Powerful and Persuasive Voice
6. Dressing for Success
7. Essential Presentation Skills
8. Giving an Elevator Pitch
9. Giving an Impromptu Speech
10. Interviewing Skills: Jobs
11. Interviewing Skills: Media
12. Job Search Efforts in the Times of Transition
13. Managing Your Online Presence: LinkedIn
14. Managing Effective Small Talks
15. Networking and Building Contacts
16. Social Media–How to Make or Break Your Life
17. Transitioning from School to Work or Vice-Versa
18. Writing a Business Plan
19. Writing a Great Op-ed
20. Writing a News Article
21. Writing a Powerful Speech
22. Writing a Statement of Purpose
23. Writing Good Recommendation Letters

| Appendix IV |
List of Contributors

●●●

History and Philosophy & Epilogue

Hungsoo S. Kim, *Korean*
President, Center for Asia Leadership Initiatives
MPA, Harvard Kennedy School of Government

John Lim, *Canadian/Filipino*
Yonsei/Fletcher, Harvard Extension School

●●●

New Perspectives

Zhoulai Zhu, *Chinese*
Ed.M., Harvard Graduate School of Education

Margaret McKenzie, *American*
MALD, Tufts Fletcher School of Law and Diplomacy

Raymond Ko, *Hongkonger*
PhD, Harvard University

Rachel Loh, *Malaysian*
MPP, Harvard Kennedy School of Government

Karol Mark Yee, *Filipino*
Ed.M., Harvard Graduate School of Education

Nikki Skovran, *American*
MBA, Harvard Business School

Paul Yoo, *American*
Ed.M., Harvard Graduate School of Education

Zach Przystup, *American*
MALD, Tufts Fletcher School of Law and Diplomacy

Lars Ragnar Aalerud Hansen, *Norwegian*
MA, Tufts Fletcher School of Law and Diplomacy